D1482833

THE
Rarest Bird
IN THE WORLD

• The wing of the *Nechisar Nightjar* •

THE
Rarest Bird
IN THE WORLD

The Search for the *Nechisar Nightjar*

VERNON R. L. HEAD

PEGASUS BOOKS

NEW YORK LONDON

Dedicated to

Ian Sinclair, Gerry Nicholls, Dennis Weir

and

The Cambridge University Expedition Team of 1990
(Will Duckworth, Mike Evans, Roger Safford,
Mark Telfer, Rob Timmins and Chemere Zewdie)

• • •

THE RAREST BIRD IN THE WORLD

Pegasus Books LLC
80 Broad Street, 5th Floor
New York, NY 10004

First Pegasus Books hardcover edition March 2016

ISBN: 978-1-60598-963-1

10 9 8 7 6 5 4 3 2 1

Printed in the United States of America
Distributed by W. W. Norton & Company, Inc.

CONTENTS

CHAPTER ONE
EMBOSSED AND SINGING

EYES ARE FOR SEARCHING, and sometimes the search is for eyes in the night. I blinked, turning my cheeks to the dusty mud. Shapes slid before me, slicing like the shadows from a tent, stealing bits of shine.

It was an elemental evening in Ethiopia. We were following a map, and it was my turn to aim the spotlight as we drove, looking for a bird of the night. Mammal eyes shine silvery, but night-bird eyes shine in warmer colours. Swollen with dreams, we were journeying enquiringly along a bumpy, beautiful track on a path through time. Stars became scribbles of direction and instruction. Time wobbled in the spot-lit air, and all was an ebony mist on the flat plain.

The sparkle from my bulb attracted all manner of flying things, except for the nightjar we had come to see. Quiet bats dodged my head predictably. Insects attacked and zapped, wedging incessantly into the recesses between my teeth. Their taste cracked, tangy and fruity in sweet, slippery movement. I spat incandescent strands that tied me fleetingly to the earth. All about me the grass was bleached in light. My stare was fixed on the moving spot that bobbed in front of our four-wheel drive, probing the dark. Not even the wiggling of flying ants and moth-like things trapped in my pants and vibrating in my groin could distract me.

This was no ordinary place. It was an in-between place; the mountains on both sides were the fresh blue of night, distant yet also close by. Named Nechisar, or 'white grass' in Amharic, the old language of the place, it was full of the vulnerable whiteness of the young, the new and the untouched. It smelt and felt of colours that were new. And it promised to change my life.

Ethiopia smiles and cries at once. Its landscape talks of primordial light and primordial movement. It has low, hot areas and incredibly cold, high areas. It is lush in some places and stark in others; it is plentiful in the birth of things, yet barren in the stillbirth of others. Here the tame and the feral mingle. There is feasting but also starvation. Some languages here sing happily while others scream in anger. Yet I found Ethiopia to be a kind host, patient and wise, although filled with many, many moods: my own and those of others and also of the landscape – even the rocks had moods.

At 1100 to 1650 metres above mean sea level, time floated like a bird, changing yet still, and always born new. Here the meaning of 'mean sea level' came into its own, speaking of the connection to the distant sea, the movements of continents and oceans, the vast scale of planetary proportion and perspective – and our smallness, our ultimate significance and insignificance. We were far beyond the reach of the tame, among undiscovered Darwinian secrets, beautifully old and African.

'Eyes!' I said.

The eyeshine came from near the ground, a uniquely paired glow of golden copper-red, bright little balls hovering side by side in the air. We were on the edge of a famous, primitive plain, at the edge of its shape, and a strange bird was sitting motionless before us like a teardrop, unsettled and temporary, not far from a large bush, all verged and edgy.

*

Twenty-two years earlier, on 6 July 1990, an expedition of scientists from Cambridge University had arrived on these plains, tucked between the hills of the Great Rift Valley. The team – Duckworth, Evans, Safford, Telfer, Timmins and Zewdie – had come to Ethiopia to find answers in and of its wilderness, and to share the mistakes of their own trammelled world so that Nechisar could remain untrammelled. They understood the meaning of the pristine in a global landscape, where ice from a peak waters flowers in the valley, where rivers become the sea, butterflies become pollen, trees become air, and a foaling zebra feeds the soil with its afterbirth juice and the cheetah with its flesh.

These long lines of interconnectedness meant that the discovery of a dragonfly in Africa was important for the sunshine in London, and so a bird's wing found by chance in the sand was a treasured object to them, a moment of celebration, and even a declaration of hope for people.

These scientists were modern in their approach to Nechisar and nature. Yet their gaze had originated in the Victorian Age, the Age of Discovery, a time of naturalist explorers whose mission it was to seek out and catalogue life in colonial adventure.

In 1836, the British survey ship HMS *Beagle* returned to England after five years circumnavigating the Southern Hemisphere, having stopped at many, many places, many seas and many islands. It had harboured a paying guest named Charles Darwin, a man of wild schemes and careful thoughts who became, over the course of the journey, the ship's naturalist. Floating up and down on the tide in the port of Falmouth, the HMS *Beagle* was aglow with his curious cargo: a vast collection of vertebrates, invertebrates, marine organisms, insects, fossils, rocks, plants, birds, and many, many new names, all richly illuminated by his thorough, careful notes and recollections of sightings, habitats, distributions, colours and sounds. On this long and important journey, Darwin had come to a new understanding of the intense variety in the natural world, and the mystery of natural selection began to evolve into answers on his quiet tongue.

On the Ross Expedition to the South Magnetic

Pole between 1839 and 1843, the assistant surgeon on HMS *Erebus*, Joseph Dalton Hooker, collected and labelled for Kew, finding new flowering plants, mosses, liverworts, lichens and algae. He named creatures and places, and found answers to island mysteries through island ecology. His profound ordering of the natural world became a part of the journey of the new scientists of Nechisar. On the HMS *Rattlesnake* en route to New Guinea and Australia from 1846 to 1850, the young assistant surgeon Thomas Henry Huxley had netted, dissected and studied the ocean creatures, describing new marine invertebrates. The oceans began to live in tiny and translucent species, wobbling like jellyfish, linking different peoples in aboriginal truths at the edges of new lands. His careful watching, drawing and noting also became part of the journey of the new scientists of Nechisar. And on the 1848 voyage of the small trading barque HMS *Mischief*, its high sails filled with strong winds and hopes, Alfred Russel Wallace and his friend William Henry Bates had sailed modestly and unofficially from Liverpool to Brazil, to its great sea of trees and new creatures and specimens.

This was a time of capturing and killing, of skinning, preserving and displaying; appropriate for that time and for that way of seeing. It brought a whole new understanding: that an uninterrupted forest of species becomes a sea of species that leads to diversity and new life. And so emerged the greatest idea in the history of human thought. It was a long journey through forests all over the world, a journey of many ships – often lonely ships, dangerous ships, burning ships and sinking ships – always collecting, always filled with forests of specimens and oceans of thoughts.

But now, to the call for knowledge through discovery and collection, the new scientists of Nechisar added the call for conservation. The tradition of unlocking the evolutionary truths of our past was overshadowed by the urgency to protect the evolutionary truths of our future. The new scientists strove to protect and preserve. They did not take needlessly from Africa, but gave instead, in the hope that tomorrow might at least be like today and perhaps even like yesterday.

These were my kind of birdwatchers: daring, gentle, empiric voyagers, emotional and intellectual explorers linked through a shared love of wilderness. They were salted in biodiversity and pushed by foreign winds, purposeful drifters on new currents; Arcadian hunter–collectors. Hunting was the act of searching rather than stalking. Theirs was a zoological farrago; they were sailors on the picturesque landscapes of Wordsworth and Coleridge, on the untamed and the beautiful. They were not just scientists but also aesthetes and poets infused with naivety; dreamers but also doers. They were painters of a picture of the whole of nature; they were Darwinii on a great sea.

The Cambridge University Expedition of 1990 lasted three months, and through day and night observations – spot-counts, transects, habitat surveys, netting, trapping, collecting and sampling, as well as caring and thoughtful writing – Nechisar became known to science.

The engagement of these scientific eyes with the wilderness was fertile in ideas yet disciplined in the gathering of facts. Just as a seed pushes a flower searchingly towards the sun, so these enquiring minds unravelled storylines from their discoveries, so that untold secrets buried in mud could emerge into the light to bloom bright and new.

They found 38 large mammal species including 9 leopard sightings and an important population of Swayne's hartebeest under threat of extinction; 23 small mammal species including a rodent and a bat new to Ethiopia; 315 species of birds, 69 butterfly species, 20 dragonfly and damselfly species, 17 reptile species, 3 frog species, and numerous plants.

They also found the wing of a bird – a small, solitary wing – which they packed into a brown bag, little guessing that this lone wing was to become bigger than any other: the most famous wing in the world! It was a wing that bridged science and birdwatching, the past and the present. It gathered people and debate, sparked imagination and dreams, and became a map to explorers, like sails to a wooden ship, setting a route for those who search out the past. This small wing was to become my own personal story of birdwatching.

On the evening of 3 September, the Cambridge team had been crossing the plain looking for nightjars. Their driver was Hans Bayer, a German expat in his Mercedes Gelundewagen, an old car left behind in Ethiopia by a traveller. This was no new big-budget expeditionary car like those seen on flashy television channels, but rather the authentic kind, appropriate for the new scientists, the kind that is happened upon during an expedition, that is part of the place, like the wood gathered for a campfire. They had spontaneously befriended Hans in Arba Minch, a little town near the Nechisar National Park, and then suddenly decided that this was a good evening to explore the deepness of this special place, because the weather called for it. It was a place with unknown recesses that held questions and much excitement. On an expedition, the night holds secrets, and scientists are drawn to its blackness like the suck of warm air in the summer dusk rising softly along a slope, talking into the evening, rustling leaves and light as it sings and murmurs inquisitively to the dark.

It was 'nightjar weather'. In their abundance, the night birds hid the starlight intermittently, making the sky twinkle like shutters on a trillion cameras. The Cambridge scientists were driving slowly down an old smugglers' track when they stopped dead. Squashed into the dry mud was a nightjar. 'Flat-life' they called it flippantly, joking being a way for concerned conservationists to make road kill feel less wasteful and pathetic, especially on the quiet roads of wild Africa. Someone jumped out and pulled the bird from the ground, leaving its shape stamped in the sand as a memory. Its body disintegrated, the feathers lifting and blowing away, lost to the warm breeze. But one wing remained intact.

The team had a policy of collecting road kills as voucher specimens to help expand their species list and confirm the identification of living night birds, which were often difficult to resolve and therefore difficult to prove. Then the eyes of a distant mammal shone up front and the group continued forward. The wing lay in a bag, untagged and gently tossed by the bouncing of the vehicle.

The next morning they examined the wing. In the dawn light it looked foreign, detached. It was beautiful, as all wings are, perfect and streamlined, clearly made for air, not for mud. Its dark browns of the night were now a softer auburn and the blurred patterns had become emarginations, patterns that spoke like words on a page. But they could match it to nothing in the documentation on nightjars, and it was nowhere described in the literature of ornithology. The wing was strangely new and foreign.

Distraction and puzzlement held the group in discussion in the morning heat. The camp table was soon scattered with papers and notes, overlapping and sliding like scales on a fish out of water. There were no decent field guides to reference, but they had Jackson's new key to Afrotropical nightjars, which should have solved the little problem immediately. But no. Coffees got cold, a sparrow sang outside annoyingly and a Marabou Stork made a shadow jump on the wall of the tent, irritating the conversation.

Roger Safford scratched his head. 'I can't make the large wing-detail fit anything. And it's bigger than any species we see here.' The question hung in space.

'This happens all the time when you visit odd places,' someone replied. 'Perhaps Jackson's key has a mistake or we're misunderstanding it.'

The marabou lifted its shadow from the tent. The group scribbled 'pending' in their logbook, put the wing in a bag labelled 'Giant Nightjar' and went to eat breakfast.

The expedition continued into more days, stretching to weeks and then months as time laboured on. Days in Africa are wide under a high, slow sun. To live under that sun is to be eternally hot, and to work under it is heavy. When eventually the day arrived of their return to England, the wing lay silently among their luggage, forgotten safely in a bag, protected quietly by indifference. Rob Timmins had preserved it on that very first morning with all the skill of a gold sarcophagus maker.

When the team left Ethiopia, however, no export permits were granted, and a pile of specimens – many small mammals, a lark and some wings – remained behind in a dark room, claimed by the city of Addis Ababa. It was a busy and confused city of many people and many lost things. This was the era of the Mengistu regime, an oppressive time: borders were tight; everything was shut like a breathless lung, like a body alive in a coffin. The innocent wing lay jailed in a room of forgotten things, trapped like time itself. Documents were copied and copied again; white paper turned yellow and time got stamped officially on forms like coffee stains. For almost a year the travel rules held and Ethiopian time stood still.

Finally Chris (Jesse) Hillman of the Wildlife Conservation Society was cleared to carry the package to London by hand. His journey was long and selfless, but at last the specimens reached the British Natural History Museum at Tring.

A natural history museum is a special place. This is where science meets the people of the streets; where a schoolchild might stare at a life-sized plastic dinosaur and imagine the past, or see stuffed birds from all over the world and dream of watching them in the air. It is an island of wilderness enclosed by a city, like a shoal of fish herded and captured by dolphins – reshaped and transformed for convenience. It is nature artificially paused, posing quietly on display to make dreams, a place of rare encounters with rare things, a celebration of diversity, a meeting of the feral with the tame. It is a monument to the age of Hooker, Huxley, Wallace and Darwin, but also to our new age, because it can be added to; it can grow like a city and expand through modern mutations, retaining its history yet gaining a new history. It can be filled with new specimens, new stuffed species, new feathers and wings. It is a monument to collection and classification; a powerful cultural cathedral of logic interpreted both physically and tangibly. It is a lavish place of displays and dioramas and dead birds in glass boxes. It is an ornate icon, a beautiful educational view of the wilderness, talking of wild mystery, telling of a way of seeing nature by naming things. It shows a way through the once forbidden woods and misunderstood denseness towards new trees and new forests at the edge of all known places – those that waited for the ships of discovery long ago and those that continue to wait.

Today's natural history museums – often physical additions to the museums of yesterday – are new exhibitions where scientific excellence radiates through new types of microscopes, where spreadsheets spew facts and data light up on screens. The new halls and wings help us to identify our place in time and in nature and our interconnectedness with the millions of other species, while also reminding us of new species. In the public areas television sets burst with accessible interaction, and wild stories are told creatively to reach the people of today – people of emails, internet and social media, of quick things and quick facts. But at the back of these museums, behind the displays, the drawers and glass boxes of birds, beyond the stuffed, dried or pickled creatures, new science is taking place.

Museums still catalogue and name; they still serve as repositories of science, but fundamentally they are home to the pioneers who search the wilderness for our lost past and our lost future, reminding us of the importance of the pristine. The museums of today share a message of preservation as we watch wild forests become suburban gardens and towns become cities. They have become conservation tools; they talk of the resilience of wilderness. These museums have become my notebooks, my bird books, my field guides, my travel guides, my maps to birds.

In the museum at Tring in Hertfordshire that morning, the wing was placed at last in front of John Ash, an independent expert on Ethiopian birds. He was mystified. Not having been on the expedition, he called Mike Evans, a team member who had just recovered from malaria and hepatitis – proud, exotic souvenirs of Africa.

'I think this could be big,' he told Mike. 'And I'm not talking about size.'

The expedition team gathered once more and stood looking down at the wing. Its tangibility was a powerful call to the heart, a revelation to the mind. The coffee suddenly tasted Ethiopian, brewed like a tribal trick, the old rooms of learning brightened, the red brick walls looked like fresh, untamed soil and the warmth felt strangely sub-Saharan. They were transported in that moment into a night on the Nechisar Plain as they imagined the glide and lift of the bird that belonged to this mysterious wing.

Questions formed, knowledge was stirred, and a task spontaneously ignited and began licking through the shelves of facts. Drawers of information crackled; responses were gathered. Excitement fuelled debate and a thorough search for numbers, sizes and empirical truths – a meticulous journey temporarily detached from all emotion, art or poetry. Roger, John and Will measured nightjar wings: every single nightjar wing they could find everywhere in the world. They measured patterns. They measured marks, blotches, strips, stripes and dots. They measured feathers and wing-patches. And then they measured and re-measured again.

Mark Telfer looked at the wing again. Then the leading British nightjar authority, Nigel Cleere, looked. New Zealand expert extraordinaire on African nightjars, Des Jackson, checked and rechecked his nightjar datasets collected over many years from museum birds across the world.

The wing was unique.

A new question emerged. Could a new species be named based on a single wing? Roger's question filtered through walls and halls, through the old wings and new wings of museums.

Worldwide, experts responded. François Vuilleumier and Mary LeCroy, eminent taxonomists from the American Museum of Natural History, were loud in affirmation and support. The editor of the *Bulletin of the British Ornithologists' Club*, David Snow, raised his thumb to the sky. High above the museum, where roofs gave way to courtyards, gardens, fields and trees, a skein of geese cut a V in the cold sky of an arriving winter. It was a change of season, a change of mood, a new state of things. Was the V for Victorian?

Within the museum, the talk was vigorous and the analysis intense. Excitement oozed from near and far; telephones rang and emails flew. Here in the past, bird species had been described from ancient remnants. In other museums, species had been described from sub-fossil remains of birds never seen, birds that had lived in a different time. A well-preserved wing from a year-old expedition presented no problem to science. A decision was made by the expedition team. Scholarly confirmation resounded in the halls and wings, and international science unanimously endorsed the claim.

A scientific paper was prepared. The expedition team of 1990 named the bird the Nechisar Nightjar, *Caprimulgus solala: solus* meaning only, *ala* meaning wing. The paper was submitted to *Ibis*, the journal of the British Ornithologist's Union, and the discovery accepted.[1]

The new species was announced, and birdwatchers like me began to dream.

---

1 R.J. Safford, J.S. Ash, J.W. Duckworth, M.G. Telfer & C. Zewdie, Nechisar Nightjar, *Caprimulgus solala*. Ethiopia: Nechisar Plains, Gamo Gofa Province. *Ibis*, 1995, 137 (3), pp. 301–307.

CHAPTER TWO
AMESEGHINALEHU ADDIS

As I STEPPED FRESHLY OUT into Addis Ababa, the stairs from the airplane swayed and the East African air whooshed up like water. I moved on a tide of humanity through queues linking people as hyphens link words, customs counters ushering us along for passport approvals, security booms lifting like gates. Months of preparation and study lay squashed inside my bags, along with my ever-present field guides, reference books and notebooks.

Birdwatchers embrace cities because they are, necessarily, where most birdwatching expeditions begin. Cities themselves hold birds only in parks, gardens and sidewalk trees, in building recesses and rooftops, on dams, concrete canals and drainage lines. City birds exist only as memories of wilderness; they are remnants, vestiges as obsolete as the human appendix. But for long-distance travellers, most expeditions begin on the runways of city airports, in international terminal halls and airport wings. Airports are like cultural cathedrals where we gather on the road to discovery, and so airport cities become symbols of commencement where we start to watch the sky.

As we set out for the city in a taxi to pick up our waiting vehicle, the Ethiopian capital hung like a great banner across the road ahead, greeting us with an Amharigna smile, strangely tantalising and protean. A high Coptic cross glistened like a ship's mast, golden green against a spicy grey sky. The air was chalked in clouds like waving white flags as if a phantom crowd was cheering. It was a special time.

We were the Sinclair Expedition of 2009: Gerry from New York, Dennis from Belfast, and Ian and I from Cape Town. Under the leadership of Ian Sinclair, the most famous birdwatcher in Africa and author of over twenty books, we had come to find the other wing of the Nechisar Nightjar, or perhaps a pair of living wings...

Everywhere people were selling fruit and talking. 'Ishee faranji,' they welcomed us. The Amharic language was rich and pulpy, like the juice of a foreign fruit plucked fresh from a tree in a wild place – sticky to the tongue and oddly delicious. It played in twists and gushes of air, and we gulped as we tried to mimic it. The sounds were zesty and athletic, sucking but not spitting, recognisable only in a lip dance of fellowship and tangy grins.

A vast billboard of Haile Gebrselassie exploded in bright red, green and yellow, framing half our view. This was the land of the greatest runners on earth, and the scent of competition lingered seductively; all was curved like muscles and fruit. Adidas, Nike, Puma – universal words of sport, western, foreign but also local – pounded the skyline rhythmically. All around us the heady cram and push of people goaded the traffic; cars hooted in cheeky taunts and we felt the challenge rise. We had a great distance to cover and a bird to find. We had been only a few hours in this new land and already I felt I was running on an Olympic track. I was thrilled, but I could not hide a distant dread. A boyhood image of a Sports Day warm-up came to mind, the most exciting and scary day of my life till then, with sharp-smelling Deep Heat burning my muscles, and a thrush screeching across the freshly mowed field, all sticky with dew and lawn-chalk in the early summer light.

Addis Ababa is new and renewing all the time. The name Addis means 'new' in the tongue of the Shewan kings, the founding kings of the place. The city had only emerged in recent times, blossoming on this escarpment of African hills. Just over a hundred years had passed since the legendary, proud and unconquerable Emperor Menelik II descended from the Entoto Hills and built a Great House on a nation of hills layered above hills. And so a gathering and a togetherness of culture resonated among the hills in that landscape amid the murmur of people and the stirrings of city-making. There was a communal licking of the fresh earth, a penetration of people into the pristine, a branding of civilisation on wilderness. It was a place where Africa was at once wild and tame.

Ababa means flower. Here, where the hot springs of Filwoha bubbled beneath flowering mimosa trees, Empress Taitu once bathed, and a city slid from her like a wet newborn child. It was a city of deceiving titillation and the bloom of growth: colours and aromas flowered in abundance in a new landscape. But cities are not flowers that open naturally and live within nature; instead they displace, pushing nature to their outer edges. There is no give and take with their natural surroundings, instead they expand like foreign, parasitic things that continue to take, banishing the wilderness as once they banished lepers.

It was still early dawn when we reached the Ghion Hotel, set in a green garden in the middle of the city, where our vehicle awaited us, shivering like a naked boy about to step into a bath. The dawn light felt like an opening, like the turning of a page. Leaning over the hotel entrance way was the green-black silhouette of a large tree alive with birds. It was a complex cut-out of a tree against the sky, a lonely symbol like a road sign. I lingered. Little city birds bounced fluffily through the leaves, all calling, disorganised and almost free, making city music: the music of the wilderness of long ago. Then, on a low, heavy limb, three large bumps moved. I had mistaken them for wood in the dark.

'An incantation of ibises!' I announced proudly, the spontaneous invention of collective nouns for birds being a new hobby of mine.

Three Wattled Ibises sat perched in the tree. For all of us but Ian, this species was a 'lifer': a bird we had never seen before, only dreamed about and studied; a number on our list, a name to be collected as a precious memory. Lifer is a big word for us. It sits alongside words like rarity, extinction, even love. Seeing a lifer is a special moment, an accomplishment, the end of a particular journey and the beginning of the next, a pause in time to wonder and celebrate the diversity and fecundity of life. It is a profound moment, but fleeting.

Hunched in the warmth of their huddle, the ibises watched us as we finally climbed into the car. And a climb it was: this was one of the old, high models, practical, spacious and heavy. It dated to a time before off-roading was easy, before clever aerodynamics and lightweight designs. Appropriately, it was from the same time as the scientists of Nechisar. It was a strong box and I liked it. The seats looked clean and felt like leather, yet warm as if someone had slept on them overnight. I was excited.

Arriving in a new city and then leaving it right away is like leaving an unfinished plate of food, a story partly untold. It was a Sunday and a public holiday, a religious day, a fasting day, and the early streets were unusually empty, except for the trees.

Addis Ababa is a eucalyptopolis, I decided as we drove along. Australian eucalyptus trees squeezed through holes in the concrete pavements and frilled on the urban outskirts until they slowly gave way to the dust of the surrounding countryside. King Menelik had planted these straight, fast-growing trees when he descended from the forested plateaus to colonise the city. They make the city softer and more comfortable; they make low things seem lower as they define routes in swathes, shadows and vertical shafts of light. The hard, tired buildings and the trees seem to sway hand in hand like ancient couples, the living and the dead together. In the morning shadows they waved and clapped in applause as we drove out of Addis Ababa into the dust.

The sounds of the city birds were soon lost to our ears as we headed south. The landscape warmed. Ahead lay a two-day drive to Arba Minch, a small town in Ethiopia's far south-west, our base from which to enter the Nechisar National Park and search out the Nechisar Nightjar. Such was our plan. From our research, we expected a safe and trouble-free journey.

The descent from Addis was subtle; my ears popped as we entered East Africa's Great Rift Valley, and then there was a slow levelling of the road. Birds – the watching of birds – always connects me with ancient things: the ancient land, the pristine past of living things, the past of people, our origins, the meaning of sentience and sapience. As we descended into the valley, a black-and-white Pied Crow glided ahead of us, following the road. Against a white cloud its white breast disappeared, detaching the wings and head from the body to drift independently like bits and pieces, like evolutionary parts, reminders of the bones and fossils scattered along the Rift Valley, memories of us, links in our story of dinosaurs and birds, and reminders of constant onward change.

This southward-winding valley of old rivers and old lakeside sediments has offered up great discoveries to humanity, gifts that reveal the history of our species and unwrap the knowledge of our departure as vigorous Africans a hundred thousand years ago, out across Africa and beyond. In time this valley became the route out of Africa, a route north into Eurasia, the Far East, thence into Australia and eventually all around the world. Now we were heading southwards towards the past, hopefully towards new questions and new answers, and birdwatching was part of our journey to understanding. As we headed down along the valley, other roads fed into ours like tributaries and all became indissoluble like veins leading to a heart.

That first morning was exhilarating. The horizon began to crackle with light. The morning sun lay like a bright, crumpled ball of wrapping paper peeled by a child from a new toy, bumpy lines of pink and orange vibrating with colour. On the opposite side of the road the sky tore long, flat lines in purples, blues and blacks. And above us hung a pure white cloud in a wall of ripples.

Unusual trees poked up out of the plain like party-favours. Deformed branches reached out, contorted with pinioned ends and pruned leaves. Boughs were hobbled and tips cut. Fields were oddly geometric, squashed rhombic boxes and scatterings of clipped grass. Ponds contained only the stains of water once held; nothing left to feed the thirst of the trees and grass. It was a fallow time, and the discipline of agriculture showed itself: low stone walls and dusty brush-framed rooms; ancient farming methods shaped by understanding and patience.

Farmscapes sit on fences of compromise between city and wilderness, between the tame and the wild. Farms are fake nature, entirely dependent on us for their greenness. Trees are constrained in lines; rivers stopped by concrete to form dams; lands quilted into pastures, meadows and crops. The living systems are dismembered like the Pied Crow against the cloud, extracted from their interconnectedness and interdependence. The planted harvest may be necessary, but it is a sad abstraction of the pristine. If you linger long enough in a quiet corner of an orchard you can hear a distant longing, a cry for the irregular, the random, the untrammelled freedom.

Yet it was on a farm that birdwatching first came to me. My grandfather's small farm on the edge of Johannesburg was a place of vegetables, flowers, ponds, avenues and orchards, of manicured life and outside dining. In the giddy time of toddlerhood when stepping and walking is difficult and everything seems very tall, my grandfather and I made our way towards the sound of a bird in the mist of an afternoon. It was the beginning of evening, the time when the air becomes crisp and the leaves on great bushes become wet and cold and slippery. The mist made me only half see the bushes, so I listened more than usual, was more obedient. The birdcall came to me on the mysterious wet mist. It was a simple, long hooting sound, stretched and repetitive like the sound of a steam engine in one of my cartoon films, making it easy to remember. My grandfather's hand rested on my head as he steered me gently through the wetness to where a giant black-and-copper bird leaned forward, bending a giant wet bush. The bird and its eyes were a fantasy of red, and it smiled at me with the crack on the side of its mouth as only a bird can smile at a child.

'Rainbird,' said my grandfather. 'Now the rain will come; the garden and the fields will be greener.'

As we left Addis further and further behind us, the in-between world of farms began to fade into a world beyond people. And along the way, as always, sometimes high in the sky above, sometimes on the roadside, there were birds. The morning light made wonderful gestures and movements, and our car-view framed a moving picture. Before noon could hide the shade, the cool blues and bucolic pastels played and pushed a pastoral bird across the road. We moved over to the side and used birdwatching as an excuse for Gerry to relieve himself. Ian, Dennis and I walked off to look for the bird. It had landed in a stunted fig tree on the verge of the fields not far from the car. Rural birds are friendly; they have forgotten much of their wildness, particularly in Ethiopia where eating wild birds is frowned upon. We walked closer to the fig tree, beating the dust from our faces, beating it out of the air before it could settle on us like mist.

'Barbet,' said Dennis.

'Black-Billed Barbet,' said Ian.

'Lifer,' said I. And I grinned.

As I watched the bird disappear, the dust undulated around me and the Great Rift Valley became for me a sea of new things, wildly tangible and wildly physical. I was on it and in it, driving along this geographic trough of new worlds and places of discovery: Eritrea, Ethiopia, Kenya, Uganda, Rwanda, Burundi, Tanzania, Malawi, Mozambique. Many millions of steps have plodded this ancient peopled passage, this deep, tectonic north–south slash extending through patient aeons as the land moves in incremental certainty. The slow movement of this place has sculpted the face of Africa with all the power and violence of a decorative tribal scar, a warrior scar. Yet on a map this proud African landmark takes on a graphic elegance, meandering indolently like a colossal, lazy serpent stretched out and sunning itself in the primordial heat. I thought of the giant ancient map of southern Africa, now famous among birdwatchers, created by the French explorer and naturalist François Le Vaillant for Louis XVI, and of its many rivers leading to the sea, its hundreds of place names, and its miniature paintings of the exotic plants, creatures and birds he encountered. And I felt the full meaning of his words. 'I breathed,' he wrote, 'for the first time in my life, the pure and delicious air of freedom.'

We proceeded along the wide, winding serpent ever southwards towards Nechisar, contained on either side by the purple shiver of distant mountains. Midday made them rock like boats on the sky. Everything was washed in dust, dreaming of water. Only lonely fig trees flushed the vistas with spots of green. And the heat began to lift eagles from trees and cliffs, until five of them were climbing and soaring above us.

I marvelled at the forces that were moving stealthily inside our earth, and contemplated the landscape in its newness and its oldness. There, written in words of stretched stone in front of us, were answers to questions about the land and its ways. Birdwatching is always about the land; it is a holistic endeavour. Finding a bird involves learning everything about its constantly changing world. The invigorating gathering of facts and clues about a bird and its place in the natural system of things helps to describe it before one finally sees it. A bird's place tells much about how it will look, how it might sleep, how it might wake. It can tell us where and when it might wake; how, where and when it might mate; where and how it might look after its young; what, where and how it might eat; what it might sound like and why; and how it might move and to where. Like the five eagles wrangling above us that day, my questions soared high and answers tumbled about.

A row of trees (planted, or merely following an unseen waterline?) shuffled in the breeze, teasing the birds that wanted to land on them. These were the only trees about. There is convenience in high trees for birds; the air is probably bouncier there, more aerodynamic. Birdwatchers are always inspecting the landscape for clues. A habitable wild place resounds in stories of life. Those new to birdwatching often speak of habitat as a concept tumbled from a book, detached and factual; a descriptive paragraph squashed beside a map or a picture of a bird. But this is only the beginning. To see a bird we must enter its habitat completely; we must connect emotionally.

Now, like the charts of the earlier explorers, habitat was the matrix. The wild world of birds led us along through Ethiopia in wing-beats of unison and debate along a plotted course that transected the new and the pristine. To find our bird, we had to find its tree. To find its tree, we had to find the land of the tree. To understand the earth, we had to learn to read the shapes of mountains and valleys, the shapes that had shaped the bird, that spoke to us of rejuvenation and constant change.

There is great romance in this journeying and finding and sharing. I thought with admiration of the great explorers of the past, and of the Cambridge Expedition Team of 1990 – of their naming, describing and unlocking of secrets. There are also the aberrant explorers: the extreme sports people raising money for charity by climbing high mountains, kayaking around continents or running coast to coast, with all their merchandising, T-shirts and motivational speaking. I thought of the first person to 'walk the Amazon', his 860 days of not looking, not seeing the trees above him or the forest floor below, not watching the ants. For me the hero was his guide, who dreamt of seeing the sea for the first time, seeing what was at the far end of the river, seeking a new view, a true discovery, a new connection.

'Is that volcano smoking?' Gerry asked.

'A cloud.'

'Put on your glasses.'

'Glad you're not navigating.'

And we laughed.

As we zipped along the slit of the Great Rift

Valley, cutting the surface of the long road, a curtain of dust floated upwards and the red land felt cracked and unsettled beneath us. Africa was moving and so were we. Nothing in nature is stationary. Even the rocks move.

We arrived at a cliff face of chalky stone. At its base was tree food: hard rock that had been crumbling for millions of years into rich soils. The roots of the trees sucked it in, networks of fungal hyphae licking like tongues and grabbing like fingers in symbiogenesis.

And from this dry woodland grew birds and nesting creatures that drank soothing waters from a brown lake beside it. Great slabs of land had been pulled apart here, sheer rock faces had appeared, tipped upwards and downwards by patient tugs and yanks: all sliding. The geological language was loud, the shapes strange and out of place, their appearance deceivingly permanent. Yet behind the stillness everything was moving. The long cliff held layers of memory: memories of water long ago, and of dust, ancient stories, perhaps floods of mud – all hard and sequential, once horizontal but now bent in great heaves of energy. The cliff in its many whites and muddy browns was like the pages of an unopened book viewed from the side, page upon page, tightly closed but filled with secrets.

A bird (a sparrow?) too far off to identify – brown as the earth and appropriately ordinary – hopped down the striated rock, down a shelf of books to the past. I looked out along the cliff and the valley and the wide plains at the bottom of the valley, and saw the sparrow more clearly. And then I saw the other birds. Everywhere birds were moving, their different colours and shapes like words beginning to form sentences. And as I looked up at the cliff again, at its layers like pages of a book, I saw birds intrinsically and I read.

Where the land on the plain had disappeared into a hole forty-five metres deep and plugged with dead lava, water had created Lake Langano. It was a beautiful wide brown lake, muddy and slithering, crocodile-slippery and bobbing with hippos. It was a place for us to rest, bathe, eat, sleep and dream, and also to watch birds. We walked out along the cliff edge where long ago a giant shaking of the earth had sheared the land on one side, and we entered the acacia forest that enclosed it.

The day was softening again as if the morning had suddenly come back to us, and all was flushed and warm, a little sleepy and lazy, draped in a padded softness. Trees seemed less rough, bark blurred slowly, and the birds and other little creatures fuzzed the leaves above us. In the distance a strange sound boomed, like the cannon call of an ancient ship.

That special light at the end of the day triggered an avian rush hour: beaks flicked and tails clapped; birds flitted, hopped and scurried, all dodging and weaving while the stragglers sat patiently, as if yawning, queuing to get home. It was a busy time of day for the forest birds.

Time clocked the shadows like a sundial; all pointing the same way, lengthening away from noon – and there was a stretching and a feeding. The fading heat tickled a little breeze into the air and the leaves rustled, aware of the coming of evening. I looked at my watch and imagined it to be a Victorian clock as the birds all called together like in the past.

A distant cannon boomed again. We walked on hurriedly, not wanting to miss anything, our binoculars tugging eagerly like hungry dogs. Tiny red leaves fiddled their way to the floor, floating slowly, pellucid and pretty, while gravity seemed to push them back up to the sky. But no, not leaves; these were Red-Billed Firefinches, tiny seed-eaters, wonderful and uniquely bright against the dust. The tiny dots on their flanks twinkled unusually white in the dryness, out of place in the dust. We watched attentively with scientific eyes; these birds were clearly a sub-species, very different from those in Africa's far south. Maybe too different? We made notes for Ian's next book.

Eight birds zipped through the trees, gliding sideways together; eight shiny, glistening starlings, their sheen reflecting a metallic purple-blue black no artist or photographer can ever capture, far from the vulgar, manufactured black of a polished city car. As one, the graceful shapes alighted on a branch in a row: regimental, steely and confident as naval officers. As they sat in their polished silvers with their silver-gold eyes, I longed to stroke their smoothness. Ruppell's Starlings: my 31st African starling species. Just a few more remained to be ticked off my list.

The distant boom sounded again, and Ian gazed up, scanning the cliff more carefully than usual.

'Seen something?' I asked, following his gaze.

'No... but this is where they saw that swallow a few years back.'

My notes came back to me. In November 1988, another expedition had noticed an unidentified cliff swallow among the swallows flying along the edge of this cliff. Their report mentioned that it might be the fabled Red Sea Cliff-Swallow. Finding this species would be almost as big internationally as finding the Nechisar Nightjar.

'Look for a steely-blue crown and a grey rump,' said Ian, 'and pay attention to the throat and upper-breast colour. You never know.'

Scanning the forest, though hushed and slow in the afternoon heat, we found excitement and movement. All about us was the nervous excitement of anticipation. A lizard ruffled a leaf; our eyes watched the cliff; swallows passed us one by one. Nobody spoke.

Half an hour passed. Then an hour. The cliff seemed to grow higher, my neck muscles stiffening like the cliff. Then the swallows were gone and the booming sound came again.

A giant shape appeared; a living shape, dark and sharp. Magnified perhaps by imagination, fatigue or the heat, it seemed bigger than a living thing should be – a great prehistoric creature, a fossil, a great living rock. We were on foot, standing in a game track of many diverse footprints; our own prints less delicate, less part of the texture, less necessary. We were vulnerable and out of place, and I was glad I was not first in line. A large, rocking walker approached us, its shadow moving in jerks, menacing but thrilling. The light revealed a bird. It stopped suddenly and looked at us, blinking with big eyes and big eyelashes. My neck hurt as we stared upwards; it appeared thirty metres tall, its head disappearing into the clouds, its massive bill curved like a cutlass, the shadow twisted and bent as it fell across other shapes.

'Now *that's* a beak!' said Gerry. We had found a Northern Ground-Hornbill – another lifer for me – or it had found us. Its vast blackness terminated in the pale blues and reds of a distant head, crowned in a fin-like carbuncle, while its wings took the sun and made sheen from the light. Then it boomed.

*

The sun yawned warm against my cheek as the day lifted itself and stretched its legs. My first true Ethiopian day – I had watched evening come and slept through an Ethiopian night; I was now part of its cycle. African Mourning Doves cooed their agreement on the nature of the tranquillity. There was oneness between birds and men. Then came the dawn chorus: the bird-dawn. The physical power of this cacophony is tangible on the early morning air, particularly on the edge of a forest: with a sudden push the sound turns the dark into palpable light. Sitting at the cusp of daybreak was like reading an avian music sheet. Mingled with the birdsong I imagined the lyre-like krar of Ethiopia, the azmari and bolel singers, and the tune 'Ere Mela Mela', the legendary harmony of Addis.

The dawn chorus is both enjoyable and instructive: the multiplicity of melodies exposes the forest's inventory of species, and we listened strategically, attentive for clues, for songs hidden beneath the leaves. We were learning diversity and imagining new birds while revelling in the lush exuberance of nature's most enthusiastic celebration of sound. At this interface between science and art, the dawn chorus was for us both a celebration of creativity and the recognition of biological certainty, the naming of morning creatures from music.

Then like spoor or braille, the dots on our map led us along our marked red line. The next town on our map was Shashemene. As we set out on the road, everything was long. The car creaked, metal stretched, springs bent and we were tugged forward. Then the land slipped into a flat, high day. The heat, high and strong, began to push down onto us.

'A dead horse!' said Ian. In the middle of the road stood a mule, indifferent to the approach of a long, rusty truck.

'Mincemeat,' said Gerry.

Our vehicle entered into a dance with the mule and the truck, and in the suck of the truck the animal spun, twirling and wobbling in a tragic circle, a macabre pirouette. Then, like a gust from nowhere, the great hulk steadied itself, walking miraculously as if it were a limping dancer to the other side of the road, and began to eat from the verge like a mellow hippy. It ate immediately and nonchalantly, this hippy horse, as one might eat from habit. Then a man with dreadlocks and smoke coming from his head tapped it on the thigh, but the mule lingered like a street dog near its food.

I watched the road more intensely now, with fresh thoughts of death as we drove. Roads both divide and unify, cutting yet fitting things into a new view of combined shapes. They link but separate the wilderness from the tamed, people from each other

and from the land. I love this quality of roads –
particularly African roads – and I also hate it. Roads
are essential to get to the birds, yet they also provide
access to destruction. As a boy I once walked through
high, dry reeds, crushing a path to an owl nest to
admire the chick. Returning to show my brother
the following day, I found the eggshells broken and
empty, eaten by a predator. Such is the way of roads.

All the way, the Ethiopian landscape was like a
poster, a concurrence of images, intersections and
crossroads, reminding me of the collage of torn
political posters on a wall at Addis airport, a layering
that created a random new multi-coloured poster of
half-torn scenes, half-faces and half-words – old and
new – smudged and linked ineffectually, yet at once
new, bold and unified.

Our long line through this place was a living
museum of travel and history, contrasting the made
with the unmade, all vibrating as we bumped along.
We came upon a stalled ancient cart, an extraordinary
feat of engineering that hovered on wheels of wood
beaten into shape with the flat metal of an ancient
blacksmith. I glimpsed a tail swooshing back and
forth: in front was an old horse, peaceful and content
like the mule of before, its tail bleached golden by the
sun. The cart was an ensemble of dead trees almost
still alive, hammered together almost musically, and it
creaked in little bells with the ancient dignity of long-

lost architecture. A filigree of painted patterns lined the seat on which an old man perched. Alongside banged an aerodynamic car in manufactured black with Ethiopian Grooves yelling from its CD player.

We came to Shashemene. 'I've gotta go again, guys.'

'A Gerry stop,' joked Ian to Gobeze, our driver, using his arms to sketch a road sign in the air. Gobeze was a quiet man who understood the roads and was serious about his driving. 'Can we buy coffee here?' We were tired and thirsty.

Ethiopia and coffee are synonymous. The coffee here is rich and ritual; the coffee-making ceremony lies at the core of social gatherings. Tiny cups are used and yet the coffee is generous. Its smell lingers; like the fizz of Coca-Cola it spreads a universal mood, always friendly and familiar.

We sat in a corrugated corner of the town, on the edge of its mess, like coffee granules stuck to the side of a cup. All about us lay a lazy chaos of things that would have been easy to pick up and put right. The lovely aroma in the ugly town reminded me of my poster view of the roadside landscape. We could just see the tips of long trees like pointed hats as we drank slow and deep. In a moment of strange urban sophistication, Gerry talked us through the complex flavours of the beautiful coffee of the town. Then, slowly, we began to dream of birds again.

After coffee came a crow. Ethiopia is crow country: nine crow species are at home here, two of which are found nowhere else. This one was another lifer for me, one of the two special crows on my wish list and the biggest in Africa, the Thick-Billed Raven.

On our way again, we passed a little gathering of children, and Gerry asked to stop. We had bottled water in abundance, and he wanted to hand some out. The road fizzed with loose gravel yet without dust: the rich red soil stuck like wax to the earth. It was healthy soil. This place had produced many trees and many children. Everything grew along an umbilical cord of freedom; and all was innocent of a wilderness connection. Huts tucked deep into the thicket had hidden many home births, and little ones filtered into the open, herding a chorus of even smaller children. Goats followed, mingling and bleating in a scamper of fur and horns, play-now-and-eat-later toys, cute reminders of what pets once were before the birth of cities. The smallest child cried in honest fear, the tops of her cheeks filling with tears.

Gerry started singing, and the laughter of the young ones bounced everywhere. The tiny crying girl smiled. Gerry quacked like a duck, hopped in bird jest, and ran up the road sliding like a sand lizard. He carried bottles of water, glowing and sparkling, refracting flickers of sun playfully into the trees. The little ones chased him and loved him. They took his hand and pointed to nests all around us: more toys in their exquisite playground. They knew all the birds, and we laughed in delight with them. They understood our birdwatching. A Spotted Palm Thrush laughed too. Dennis grinned; it was a new bird for him.

Time passed, and our entrance into the wildness opened into a giant smile. We were back in an acacia forest that had no end. Untamed leaves rustled softly, sprinkling bright chlorophyll dust across the distance. Every little flap of a leaf on the numerous trees, big and small, called with a comforting quiver to welcome us in, like the quiver-shiver as you slide into a warm bath on a cold night.

A wave of specks fiddled lovingly on a new breeze: a sea of brilliant green met blue in a bumpy line at the bottom of the sky. We turned through the massive leaves of a sudden banana grove, near to a bright river edged in more trees, and came upon a sign on a pole: NECH SAR PLAINS. The moment stamped itself into memory, clocked like a timekeeper's click at thirty-one minutes past four. There was a gap between NECH and SAR where the 'I' had been forgotten or dropped off the sign, and the pole was chequered in black and white.

CHAPTER THREE
THE BRIDGE OF HEAVEN

DUSK GRABBED AT THE sun like a greedy child, casting all in silhouettes as we reached the Nechisar National Park. The 'gate' was a gathering of round huts roofed in dry grass, with transparent walls of thick twigs as if fences had been stolen from the fields and bent to form homes. Did the wind never blow here? The huts bore an ephemeral grin of instability as if the architecture did not trust itself. These expectant, skeleton-like structures appeared to huddle in tribal discussion about our fate, casting stick shadows over our car like prison bars. Sharply whittled sticks staked out a path, like poisonous striped caterpillars warning hungry birds to stay away. I pressed my thumb on the tip of one and a bubble of blood appeared. Further back, a bleached lion skull glowed on a sloped roof as the sun grew feeble. Piles of irreplaceable firewood poached from the forest lay twined into transportable clumps.

Nature conservation is complicated in Africa, the land of my birth and hopefully my death. Conservation is always complicated, but in Africa it is nuanced with ritual, making it more complex, intrinsic and personal. Here the tradition of gathering around fires by night (and day) in an intimate relationship with the natural world illuminates the place of people and wild animals, holding the memory of the interconnectedness of humans and wilderness. Birdwatchers, too, sometimes gather at night around fires on the brink of a journey or at the edge of a forest.

Such moments remind us of our African origins and our primal need for wilderness.

A long time has passed since the earth first stretched and cracked, the seas widened, the lands swelled, and an island of people grew in Africa. As evolution made its choices and family fires flickered in scattered gatherings, selective pressure reduced our common ancestors to just six hundred people, squeezed through a bottleneck and pushed into a new world. Like a river becoming a delta or a tree fanning towards the sun, the primal heat of tribal fires led to dispersal, and the land made the people while the people made the land. After all this time we have to be reminded that we are all Africans by the truths unearthed through the digging and dusting away of scientists. We have to be reminded to stop, pause, watch and learn. Even among the icebergs of Greenland, the Inuit hold a deep memory of their savannah home: the icebergs are their reminders of once-forested hills, the ice fields of Africa's hot sands. A primordial craving for Africa and our pristine selves lies embedded in the humanness of us all.

Some stayed behind in that Africa where the rich brown earth became part of them. The delicate systems of life in that place sought balance and harmony, and the intimacy between that primal landscape and its people over the millennia has layered that Africa with memory and ritual.

But uneasy changes have defined a new Africa. At the hutted entrance to Nechisar National Park, as the smell of unnatural decay leaked from a hut and a slaughter-stain trickled from a wall like a tear, I stared into the knowledge of that new Africa. A great spear, a foreign spear, has been thrown into the heart of Africa. At first it pierced gently, like a scalpel curing disease, but today that spear is gilded with greed, and everywhere the talk is of oil, horns and gemstones while the colonised continent stumbles from its wounds. But wild things are resilient, and the land needs time to heal. And nature has time; nature is time.

Birds bounced through the trees of the little village at the gate, branches shook, and then a Red-Headed Weaver hopped brightly onto the lion skull to preen itself and fluff up the afternoon, before bathing in the nearby water until it shone.

A tall, uniformed man walked slowly towards us with powerful steps, heavy as an elephant, swollen with gravitas, his boots crunching officially from within themselves. He was swaying slightly in a rhythm of control, like an elephant. A shiny black beetle scurried ahead of him and he squashed it deliberately without altering his rhythm or the hollowness of his sound. A Kalashnikov machine gun extended his arm almost to the ground, its wooden butt newly homemade and stained, perhaps with blood. He had blood on his boot, and a fly followed him as if tamed like a dog. Behind him, herded by the evening dark, came three more men, also green and long-armed. They were silent, but their eyes spoke without compromise.

Gobeze got out to speak to the tall man while we hung back, enclosed by the metal skin of the car, peering out at the soldiers. We smiled to hide our nervousness as a man with a homemade machete tapped his steel blade against my window, testing us as he tested the glass, as a dog might smell another's crotch.

Gobeze was also our interpreter. We had asked him to get us onto the Nechisar Plain at night. This was against local law, and a great favour we were asking of him, a favour that held the chance of friendship. He was a responsible man and determined to help – as he had done on the long road – and we saw him reach deep into himself in the pause before he walked towards the soldiers, perhaps to change his manner from our way to that of the green men. As he searched for expression, his face found theatre and new emotion. He talked in a language we could not understand, filling the air with fun. They encircled him like pelicans on a lake, and then dipped forward in laughter, almost in the giggles of children. Gobeze flapped his outstretched arms and jumped into the sky, finding a connection with the men, perhaps reminding them of their youth, of the time of magical landscapes, wild pets, of firesides and their own connectedness;

and so he found friendship and agreement. We were permitted to proceed at night.

Our map required us to drive deep into the park. Entering without a permit might have meant death. We had had to think like politicians and military people, using words like 'protocol' and 'deploy', becoming green in the camouflage of deception rather than the camouflage of belonging. But in the end it was only through Gobeze's sincerity that we succeeded. And after the heaviness of that big, stressful moment came the curl-up-in-front-of-the-fire tiredness; the good tiredness of a busy mind and a well-worked body.

＊

Our travels had led us far from cities, far from the comfortable and the familiar. Travel is integral to birdwatchers, and we view the world as infinitely accessible. For us the places at the furthest edges of the globe await us fondly, because they are where the birds are. Birds are everywhere and we dream that we will eventually see them all, that no place will remain unseen, unwatched. We see our planet without boundaries. For us the borders of countries are ephemeral; they are merely in-between places, like hills fading into valleys, forests becoming seas, mountains holding oceans apart, days fading into night – only interconnectedness. Boundaries become real only in quick moments at airport cities.

My first birdwatching journey occurred during a summer holiday when I was twelve. It began with our school chaplain raising his arms and dismissing us to an open, free, end-of-term sky. Beyond my classroom the light was angled low but already warm and attracting bees. The freshly mowed lawn lay bright and luxurious, stretched like a road between me and the big, wide gates. Our family had planned a road trip to visit extended family members who lived in towns, on farms, on beaches and among mountains, and it included stops at some purely holiday places, all of which abounded with new birds. The road linking these stops was sometimes as green as the school lawns and wondrous for running and exploring; it was a road of birds between places of other birds. That summer I discovered over four hundred species of birds: four hundred ways of seeing, four hundred answers to questions. That first birdwatching journey lies now as a list of birds in my notebooks. Roads, maps, birds and answers have become an allegorical way of life for me. To me the names on road signs and maps are patterned like genetic codes, unlocking old memories and potential new ones (Cape Town is the Cape Canary and the Cape Sparrow; Pofadder is the Sclater's Lark; Durban is the Common Myna), forever linking habitable names with the phenotypic names of the living and the wild. And in another way, in an ephemeral, ethereal way, my birdwatching is also the navigational lullaby of the nightjar. It lives on soft dreamy, hopeful wings. The journey of birdwatching is always the journey to the bird, and along the way it becomes a journey to other journeys.

*

In the silence of Nechisar we sat tightly in the vehicle. The sunset was cool, its final flick of light pushing through a slit in the branch of an old tree on a dark hill above us. The hill was fluffy with the texture of bush, blurry at its edges in hesitant colours. I watched the tree flagging the sky, and then I slept.

Then the tree stretched down to us in a fresh shadow, and the glow from behind the hill was suddenly bright. The light from the tree cracked and burst through a hole, and pink disappeared into orange. Birds launched a million calls and flew over us in teams, gliding and flapping purposefully, the air fuzzing with their hurry to begin the day. A whole night had passed and everything was new.

Gobeze's hand shifted his seat and turned on the engine. The shudder of the car motor was soothing, like a soft stroking of the head. Fresh dew slipped down the window against my cheek, and I remembered that we had rested somewhere near the gate, then returned to the entrance gate in the blackness. The guards in their huts waved. The back door of the car opened like an involuntary yawn, and in climbed our new assistant, Bhanti – appointed during Gobeze's pelican-dance with the guards – his long gun scraping the metal side-panel. He settled on the spare wheel with his sparkling bullet belt slung across him like a garment.

The back door – hinged to the roof – closed with gravity as we jerked. Then we nudged forward through the gate and entered Nechisar. The track was just two narrow brown lines of mud framed in green: high bush on the outer sides with low bush in-between, steering us like a train track. The bushes gradually swelled into trees, then into vast walls that tilted inwards and finally touched in a darkening green that obliterated the sun. Textures turned from smooth and flat to a network of tiny rough holes where light formed leaves and green stars. We sailed this huge long tunnel like a wave, tilting gently from side to side, dipping and floating as the watery green gushed high and fast over us, and stars of light sparkled photosynthetically. The arched ceiling showed dapples of sky and glimpses of shimmering clouds in a paler, distant green behind a million sprinkles of leaves that fizzed like spray. Below us our wheels cut through the rich mud of the forest – and then the mud turned watery and we drove forward in a riverbed. The river became our way, our only way: all was water below us for a while, moving mud and little round rocks.

It was the most beautiful forest I had ever seen, perhaps in its great contrast to the world I had come from. It was a tall, lost forest, hidden in Africa, shielded by untouched mountains and rivers. It was not famous, not yet featured in Hollywood movies or sung about by pop stars like the song of the Amazon (where I have also been and learnt many things about forests), but it bore an ancient wisdom as all forests do. Perhaps its smallish size, I thought, might keep it just for me, for my exclusive 'most beautiful' claim. The forest reflected back my grin in its many pools with the freshness and innocence of the undiscovered. The trees were higher than my highest imaginings, and they brought to my mind the tree people: those who know trees, who care about trees, who can find rare trees among common ones, identify them at a glance or from their rustling in the breeze, and call out their scientific names and common names, perhaps even in different languages. Then I looked at the forest through the eyes of the birds: as holders of nests high and low in boughs and forking limbs; great tree stems promising a firm holding; wide stems offering holes and hollows; twigs and leaves for weaving and bending into egg baskets; bird food hanging and crawling and flitting among the branches... everywhere, everything was for the birds. I thought of the changing seasons of the forest and how birds tell of these changes by calling, calling differently, or ceasing to call at all; by behaving differently, flying differently or displaying the seasons on their wings. In evergreen forests especially, where green is always green and leaves do not change with the seasons – as in this forest at the entrance to Nechisar National Park – the leaves surrender their voices to the birds.

This was a watery riparian forest defined by the grip of the Kulfo River. The water was coppery, lined with coppery pebbles, and the huge trunks banked the edge, the tidal lines on their bark the same as the lines that patterned the flowing water. The roots of every tree grasped unfathomably, holding like ropes, and I pictured them writhing like snakes in a loose, bottomless liquid of black mud. The river and the trees seemed a part of each other, holding hands as they skipped and sang along together like my own twin children, separate but similar, close but independent. I wanted to embrace the trees in togetherness and tug gently at their limbs in family play.

Of all rivers, a forest river is the most exquisite, part water and part tree, a conglomeration of forest pieces that become each other. Small silver curves and frothy humps emerged in soft-sided swirls like floating cream, puffed and airy amid the green. Our forest was wrapped in a skin of water. The water moved in leaves and the trees streamed in long lengths, dripping and gentle.

The track in front of us became a deeper river. Our wheels fanned water upwards, and behind us a wake wobbled with our car-print, disappearing in white bubbles. A disturbing notion of loneliness came to me, slowly at first like a leak, as the parallel muddy tracks became wider and more watery and our link with the road became less certain. The trail faded away; our tie to safety – our rope – had run out. Now as we moved forward we left no trace of having been there, no spoor-line as we moved ever further from our homes. Then rain fell towards the sky! Rising from the ground below us in a storm, clouds and showers in drops and in tiny splashes burst from beneath the car in many colours, texturing the air with thousands of little wings of orange, pink, purple, blue, green, red, yellow, white and other colours, reflecting in minuscule mirrors an endless shoal of colours, never seen before.

And the mud on the forest floor made magic: a haze of butterflies added to the green, the first butterflies of our Ethiopia. Minerals in the forest soil had collected as a crust on the few last bits of dry track ahead of us that hinted at a route, on which many species and sizes of butterfly were now congregated, all feeding, sunning and simmering in the light while the evergreen leaves lent them their voices. We rolled along like a wave, and the butterflies and birds took to the air with us, moving up and down through the trees.

Then, gradually and quietly, the gentleness of the butterflies was replaced by tsetse flies, creatures that belong as patently as butterflies, but nearer to the forest edge to the other side. The tsetse fly is a part of so many tales of African journeys, of great armies and empires that have come and gone. Despite an often uncompromising intolerance to this fly by those who do not belong, all have ultimately had to obey its wildness, its nature of feeding, its accord with the shade and the sun, its perfect place in the landscape. The tsetse has blunted spears, muddled cow paths and disturbed tribes in its unrelenting harmony with its world. The famous Masai tribes of southernmost Kenya recall proud battles with lions but failed battles with the tsetse fly and the lethal disease it spread among their cattle and their warriors. This small fly has had a giant impact on Africa, separating areas, containing people and dispersing others, particularly cattle people. In this way it has left a legacy of discovery and travel, but also of untouched natural landscapes, protected and pristine – places to find new birds. As a visitor and birdwatcher, I thought of the importance of respecting the place visited, respecting the rules between habitat, bird and birdwatcher, and all the beautiful, undisturbed (and often inconvenient) equilibriums.

We rolled along slowly like buffalo, the shallow tree roots making our car lumber and lean. As we continued in and out of the river, through dips and higher areas between trees, in and out of the light between the many greens, the tsetse flies came to our car, determined in their elegant, instinctive way to pierce our fresh hide and feed. The car cast a large shadow, a big, flat black-box shadow that slid across the mud in bumps and uncomfortable shapes. And always the flies followed us.

Gobeze drove us onwards, shifting through his gears, shifting the tsetse flies. The windscreen wipers swished like a tail, squashing flies, leaving muddy arcs of green-red juice. The engine moaned, and at the front the bull-bar thrust forward like a horned head.

Then the forest ended, the light changed in a rush and above us the morning opened. The two parallel tracks of black mud that had led us like a train became hard brown crusts, then light brown sand, the brown of the ground lifting towards a hill.

At the edge of the forest two or three trees shook violently. It was difficult to establish where one tree ended and another began, or to see what was making great clumps of leaves shiver in the green stillness. Then the trees shrieked, and monkeys appeared, playing lightly on the treetops, teasing the sun leisurely. They were black-and-white Guereza Colobus Monkeys, familiar to us in their strangely detached manner like nuns in habits. They were a family group and hugged each other as people hug. One twirled a flower in its mouth like a cocktail umbrella, and as I watched through my binoculars its sharp white teeth snapped over the flower.

The sky was blue on the hills, its emptiness filled with a deep, pure, three-dimensional blue that moved in moods like the blue of oceans. Then a single, slow curve appeared, the streak of an emerging cloud, crystallising from a disturbance in the air currents, a vapour penetrating into the blue, hot against cold like an injection of warm blood. I saw the cloud as a sailor might have viewed a whale long ago, as a sign of life in the distance, of the deepness of life, as Captain FitzRoy might have seen it in a cry of discovery from high on the rigging of the HMS *Beagle*.

I imagined the cloud as an evolving whale, its origin a curve firmly rooted on land. If it had had an eye it would have been deep blue, smooth and slippery, edged with the rolling of tiny silver bubbles. The whale might have been 49 million years old, the most primitive known saltwater whale ever known, which lived at the edge of land and sea with its long hind legs and hands. It might look down on the hippos in the lakes as floating reflections; or back to the edges of the new hills we were now climbing and remember itself in the nimble hoofed creatures and furry creatures below. If it were a gulping whale, it might have scooped like a blue whale – the largest creature ever – sieving and sprinkling plankton-like particles in the sky. Towards this cloud a line of white cattle egrets soared, over the hills and distant plains, away over the blue.

I had read about the others before us who had found Nechisar. Here the Kori people had sowed, the Guji had herded, the Gamo had wandered and the Dorze had fought. The Ganjule had killed hippos here, the Konso made their music and the Gofa left quiet memories on the land. The first 'white' man to stand here – called 'white' only to stress his foreignness, his temporariness and the contrast of his skin with local skins – was the American Arthur Donaldson-Smith, after whom a nightjar was later named. He came in 1895 for the large trophy animals, the 'big game' as they are still called today when shot and killed as sport. I imagine that Africa's large animals, particularly the easy-to-see herbivores in their great herds on the open plains, are called 'game' because of the fun they represent for those who shoot them. Although this is not my sport, hunting as sport can and does help to save wild animals and wild places in Africa. But for Donaldson-Smith, hunting was also a form of collecting, and was made useful to early naturalists as specimens in natural history museums. Others in the past who journeyed to Nechisar or nearby also explored and named (perhaps in many languages), and much now lay on distant shelves in distant halls, graves and wildernesses, dead and alive, named and unnamed, seen and unseen.

Ahead of us, above a hill of silky brown sand, a long mountain unwound like the neck of a dead giraffe, uncurling across the earth in fossilised mud, soiled in stretching twists, and sharp-edged in a sequence of giant black vertebra-like shapes in volcanic rock. It was pointed and bumpy along its ridge, a high, loose, dangerous place where rocks crumbled constantly to become sand. This was Egzer Dilday, the Bridge of Heaven, our only route to the Nechisar Plain. It was a new mountain, part of a changing, moving mountain that meandered across a vast body of water, dividing it into two lakes. It had arisen spine-first out of the water at a time when the lakes were still one, and now it spanned the Great East African Rift Valley as a rung spans a ladder, swaying delicately in the way bridges sway, at once in-between and above, while also linking. It was a natural dam without concrete, from a time before there were people. One lake reflected back the clear blue of the sky while the other lay brown with mud and ancient sediments, reflecting the sky like brown glass or a dirty window. The blue lake was Chamo and the brown one Abaya, names given long ago, after the twin lakes birthed together as Africa widened.

The mountain was like an umbilical cord, a connection across valley-sides, feeding and growing by linking, but also separating by being in-between. It was a wet-edged isthmus of stone, wild and virile, protruding from one place and penetrating into another, and everywhere alive with the movement of birds. We climbed that strange mountain – part cliff, part pass, part track, part dream – drawing strength from it as it lifted us higher towards the Plains of Nechisar. As the vehicle heaved us slowly upwards and eastwards, Lake Abaya spread out to our left, frilled with a soft skirt of reeds, its waters evidently a rich cocktail of reed nutrients. Lake Abaya was large, its surface pierced by the tips of newer mountains – future lake-makers – forming sharp little rock islands no more than twenty or thirty metres wide and fifteen high: Aruro, Gidicho, Welege, Galmaka and Alkali, strategically arranged to display the lake's famous crocodiles – the biggest in the world. There was also a moving island, a floating, bloated island of hippos. A great Goliath Heron lifted from the water, its head erect. A fish eagle called from the clouds, appearing black and white like the crows of our first day in Ethiopia.

Gerry impersonated its shriek, stretching his arms comically like wings. 'The call of Africa!' he announced in the mock accent of a television commercial. Then he scowled at the sand hissing from the slowly rolling tyres. 'We walk faster than this,' he said. The rubber tyres seemed to pat the sand rather than rip at it.

The track was not steep; the challenge was its unstable surface. Driving over the loose, crumbling earth was unsettling, and boulders lay on the slopes about us: large, black rocks waiting to tumble, crash, crush. Looseness was everywhere, and old boulders – those that had already tumbled from above or from the cliff below – lay shattered, oozing sand. We trickled uphill like water forced to climb, while the dust made bubbles in the air and the sand jerked. Each moment of movement was a little triumph. We watched as trees grew, weaverbird nests turned from green to dry straw. Clouds overtook us like traffic. The day became long and stretched.

Progressing along that bridge of rock offered us a view from above, far out over the bush land and across to the slopes of Egzer Dilday. A scattering of shrubs and low trees stood in white grasslands that bent in gentle curves. The plants on our crossing held the mountain together in a giant rope of greens, wrapped tightly against the fertile soil. The sand was wet and shiny, and the black rock held little pools of water from the previous day's rains, little mirrors that caught bits of sky. I understood now how rain and sand could work together to give life where once there had been death.

Flat-topped acacia trees, quintessential to East Africa, echoed the lines of the ground, making the land float like wobbling air in a horizontal layer of bark and leaf. Even their shadows floated. Some of the smaller trees were old, their woody stems leaning, constrained in their growth shapes by the heavy tug of creepers. Occasionally a candelabra tree had pushed through the thicket, a rare and distinctive succulent in a place with so much water, fleshy and thick among the other leaves like arms reaching out of a crowd.

Our wheels crushed wild herbs beneath us, releasing exotic culinary aromas. The excitement made me peckish (perhaps from childhood meals in front of the television while watching rugby), and my mind now began searching for memories of food. Even the crackling grasses seemed to dress the air with sweet flavours as we pushed upwards in a delicious salad of tossed foliage.

In a small clearing lit up by a sunbeam, two diminutive dik-diks (small antelope) posed and danced while we watched, showing no fear of us. One winked and flicked its left shoulder, causing a fly to lift and circle like a bird. The fly seemed large beside these delicate dik-diks, whose legs were mere fibres balancing little bodies of hair – glowing, sunny, glamorous hair. Pointy little faces pricked the air as their hooves pocked the ground. These were Guenther's Dik-Diks, first recorded at Nechisar by the Cambridge expedition, and a new species for me to tick off (I also keep mammal, amphibian and reptile lists, as the deep relationship between all species is integral to my birdwatching).

As we continued upwards, Lake Chamo threw the

sky up at us in lovely confusion, mingling water and air, cut only by a thin distant line of white clouds. An identical image bounced up to the clouds and down to the ripples, and our view south became a Rothko painting, the colours at once reflective, translucent, washed and strangely modern. There were so many blues – Picasso's oddly lonely, melancholy blues; the blues of music; the blues of a gentle chill; the tight, proper blues of Victorian seafarers; and the dark, almost unfriendly blues of the deep ocean – every blue I had ever known was there, unforgettable and ultimate. At last Lake Chamo was no longer just an imagined, unreachable place to me.

And suddenly we had crossed the Bridge of Heaven. We had been absorbed into the timeless in-betweenness where land and sky met, where adventure pushed infinitely with a wild rhythm, where the sun became the keeper of deadlines and moments, where the land reflected long, thin shadows like the hands of a clock. The sun had led us in its full arc and we had followed. The day had been an endless instant. Ahead of us now flowed the long white grass, smooth and soft and foreign. The Nechisar Plains. It was like meeting a superstar.

'Kill!' shouted Dennis. The violence of the word punched the wind from my diaphragm as the brakes bit. We all jerked and Gerry hit the ceiling, swearing as his upper lip absorbed the imprint of his teeth.

But Dennis's word was not meant as an instruction, merely a description of the drama that was in front. An area of grass lay squashed with the imprint of a struggle. Curved bones reached from the ground in a cage, hollow like a wire sculpture framing a shape once owned by lungs. The black-and-white stripes of a zebra were glued to motionless limbs, one leg in a frozen gallop, another pointing to the horizon like a headstone. White-Backed Vultures scurried away.

'Hey!' said Ian. 'A Ruppell's.'

Silhouetted on a rib, lurking amid the stench, a large puffed shape was distinguishable from the other birds by the scaled pattern of its feathers like medieval chainmail, intensifying its illusion of aggression. Society's stereotype of the vulture is sadly superficial and disrespectful, as naïve as that of the owl as bespectacled wisdom, the parrot as tropical jester and the dove as promise of peace. The vulture is always the symbol of death. What a birdwatcher sees is elegance and grace, the swan of *Swan Lake*, a choreographed player in a perfect show. My kind of birdwatcher delights in the vulture's critical soar, its incredible stare, its feral connection to the plains of Africa. We marvel as it rips and swallows in exquisite adaptation, cleaning the landscape in a radiance of order, a vital participant in the narrative of the wilderness. In the cycle of decay and rebirth, the zebra and the vulture are one. For us, the vulture is a symbol of life.

In excitement we pushed through the grasses onto the plain as the light slid ahead of us among the shadows of vultures in a delicate race towards the horizon. Jabs of sunshine illuminated little migratory Whitchats, popped on sticks in their pretty summer colours, visitors just like us. Grant's Gazelles stood full-bellied and feeding, tails swishing in intense preoccupation, their heads hidden as they tugged. A Hartlaub's Bustard called. White-Tailed Larks flicked at each other in display flights. Whites turned to soft green-pinks as the orange lick of late afternoon stained the sky, and then the blues of evening lifted in fusion. The moon came floating in like a boat from the mist, and I looked up and tried to name the stars on the darkness. And I thought about the nightjar we had come to see.

CHAPTER FOUR
GOAT SUCKING

ON THE EVENING OF 21 April 2009, the dark was deep – a heavy, fathomless dark, like the place of sea-monsters at the bottom of the deepest sea. Light echoed only as memory, like the starlight of long ago. Distance was very deep, deeper than ever before, and in this heavy dark there was much to see and find, some things far away like stars, some close.

I was attached dutifully, purposefully, to the large spotlight; I was a part of it as I clutched it determinedly to my sticky, sweating self, dangling out of the side window of our vehicle. We were shuffling along the edge of the plain, looking for movement. In the quiet a late, lingering butterfly entered the air reluctantly, flushed out and lost among the moths.

Then distant eyes gave a sudden twinkle – catching and reflecting the light from my great torch. The eyes blinked, stirred in the distance. My body shuddered like the car, and I felt as light as the butterfly but also crushed like the rock. I had consciously cultivated a triumphant scream to use when calling out 'nightjar', a sound I thought might be appropriate at the first sighting of the rarest bird on our planet. The sound I eventually emitted was a strange, spontaneous moan of instruction. It had no time to become a word, but somehow it transcended words. Perhaps such sounds have always been with us, primordial sounds from a deep dark place inside us like the bottom of the sea, sounds of tension and discovery that pull like a rope.

The soil stirred into dust and our tyres crushed a small rock as we stopped.

With his video camera clasped in both hands, Gerry's fall was uncontrollable. With a grunt he absorbed the punch of the leather headrest before ricocheting against the ceiling. Dennis and Ian were already half out of their seats, binoculars in hand. I remained on the windowsill, wedged on the sharp slit of the door where the glass emerged, determined not to disturb the light beam that transfixed the bird. I perched above the puff of dust, above the busyness, clutching the light like the end of a shining rope, like a spider's thread dangling with its catch. My job was to direct the team onto the nightjar; theirs was to walk-stalk carefully along the edge of the light towards the bright yellow spot illuminated thirty metres ahead.

'In the centre,' I whispered loudly, with more confidence than my first strange utterance. 'It's sitting side-on next to that bush in the centre of the light.'

Now that I was stationary, the density and frequency of insects arriving at the torch was overwhelming. Instead of flying past or bouncing off me, every creature now landed at the source of the light. This abundance of nightjar food was encouraging, but alive with discomfort. I chewed and gobbed insects, I spat them and swallowed them. Ian, Dennis and Gerry needed to get closer to the bird at the end of my beam to see the distinctive features of its plumage – the patterns and colours and shapes – while taking photos and video-grabs. First prize, of course, would be to actually pick up the stationary nightjar and examine it in hand.

Bizarrely, nightjars freeze in a kind of trance in direct torchlight once you have their eyes locked onto a steady and unbroken beam, a useful trait when studying them. You can then approach and pick them up to examine them; then release them with no ill effect to bird or handler. Sadly, the same could not be said for me, the torchbearer, sitting on the swaying, uncomfortable door, on the knife-edge of the protruding glass pane, while my body sparkled spectacularly, crawling and crackling in a skin of live insects.

'Hurry up,' I croaked, bug-muffled, bug-muzzled and barely able to speak. Time pulled tighter like the tightest rope as I signed the air with my free arm, pointing urgently at the bird.

Never point at a bird.

This vital rule is known to every birdwatcher, but momentarily I had forgotten it. Blame the insects! Blame the door! In the flick of my finger the magic spell was undone. The bird leapt into the sky and all became a blur. Feathers fuzzed, the glass in the door cracked and the night snapped shut.

'It's a Donaldson-Smith's!' called Ian and Dennis together, having already focused their binoculars on the nightjar. In opening its wings it had revealed itself – and then it was gone.

This was not the bird we had come for, but it had been a good test of our skills. Months of study and preparation now came alive in us as though we had just stretched and warmed up for a big race (my bottom was now indeed well warmed and my skin well stretched). Nightjar-knowledge oozed through our veins; we were nightjar-ready.

Birdwatching is by no means a sport – it is about a new way of seeing, it is thoughtful and philosophical – but it requires practice all the same, and we had practised. We had made sure we knew everything about all the nightjars that might possibly appear in southern Ethiopia, and also plenty about the nightjars throughout the rest of Africa (25 nightjars, all with different calls and ways about them). We had spent many hours reading and learning the different plumage characteristics of all the species, and many nights watching various nightjars. We had been observing species in different habitats all over the continent. We wanted to make quite sure that if we observed something new, we would be equipped to recognise it as such immediately We wanted to be in a good position to record accurately what we witnessed. Nightjars had become our birdwatching storyline, our way of understanding the language of wings.

*

Long, long ago, in the time of ancient fields and shepherds, every evening was filled with an impenetrable darkness that allowed minds to wander and imagine. Half of every day belonged to the unknown, and with every sunset the air outside – beyond the windows, beyond the villages – became dense with mystery. Much of the land was unexplored at that time, and it lay all around in swathes, untouched and untamed. The world of people was a smaller world then. People were separated by greater distances, and distances were measured in time; the great time it took to travel these distances made them appear even greater. And the vast uninhabited spaces that filled the distances everywhere were dark like the night, and wild. In this ancient time, nature was close, surrounding every village. Curious people observed the fringes of the wilderness then and wondered about the creatures that visited from there. Some of the creatures that visited from that mysterious darkness were flyers: graceful blurs, soft, light shapes on wings in the sky. These were the vanishers – regular strangers, predictably silent, that came on a wing in the dark but disappeared into the distance before dawn.

One morning, an old man was walking among his goats like a father among a crowd of children. From the grass between the many legs of his goats he heard a strange sound. The old man pushed the goats apart, and a strange creature gaped up at him from the shade beneath them. It was a small creature with a great mouth and great eyes, and it pressed into the ground the way a large frog sits in mud. Its smallness made its eyes and mouth seem greater. Its large eyes and mouth made it seem bolder, and this boldness made it seem fierce. It made the sound of a snake, a new and threatening kind of snake. The old man had seen such a bird before in the dusk at the furthest edge of the village, but he had never known where it lived, why it came to the village from the forest, and why it came only in the night. The night bird was injured, and its wings hung down in the dew that morning, lying in the dampness, pushing down like limbs. Water had gathered in little balls on the feathers of its flat body, magnifying its brown colours through their clear, curved edges. As the old shepherd bent forward, the sound of the night bird grew louder. He looked again at its beak, which was too large for such a small creature. When the bird stretched its mouth open, it became big, dark and cavernous like the forest itself, the forest out of which the shepherd had seen such creatures fly. Its mouth was wet and shining in the light, deep and wide, and perfectly shaped for a goat teat. And then the old man knew why the mouth was that shape and why the bird had come to the village every night and was now among the legs of his goats. And so he named it the Goatsucker.

This is my own personal fairytale of the first birdwatcher and the first naming of a nightjar. It was these early inhabitants of small pastoral villages, living at the edges of the fragile bubble of civilisation – where paddocks and pastures became forests, where paths dwindled into lonely tracks – who watched and discovered and began to name. This naming linked the new birdwatcher and the new bird – the Goatsucker. The name became part of the language of the village, part of the story of the village and the forest, and a connection to another world that became part of our world, linking two separate worlds to make a new world.

Names belong to communities, and names become a way of seeing the named thing. Other communities that saw or heard the Goatsucker gave it other names. Some called it the Flying Toad; some called it Lich (corpse) Fowl; some called it Night Raven or Night Crow. In Germany they called it Ziegenmelker; in Spain, Chupacabra; in Italy, Succiacapre; in ancient Greece, Aristotle named it Caprimulgus or goat-milker. Others called it names I will never know.

In the beginning it was not watched with joy, with the eye of the aesthete, the hobbyist, the scientist or the environmentalist. Birdwatching began from a need for control, from concern and from fear. At first the Goatsucker was seen as a religious abomination, as evil. People looked to wild creatures for usefulness; to feed upon them in every possible way. When watching and observation found no usefulness, they cast the creature into a role within their belief system, perhaps as another kind of usefulness. The Goatsucker was not food, so it fed superstition. It became a source of fireside stories: instead of flying it roamed the sky; instead of pecking it drank; instead of perching it hung from goats and sucked. While swallows soared by day, the Goatsucker dangled poisonously at a tit by night. Where pigeons marked cobbled streets and squares, the Goatsucker dripped and stained and infected.

And yet nightjars do not suck goats. At last the scientific community – namers of the creatures collected by the early explorers who looked enquiringly at the new edges of our world – named it the European Nightjar, describing where the bird occurs and the jarring sound it makes at night.

Nightjars of many types began to visit our world as sparrows do, and became accepted as part of the rich diversity of bird shapes, colours and sounds. And again, people looked to them to find usefulness. Nightjars became used as important indicators of the health of the environment, of temperature changes in the climate, of the cleanliness of the air, the freshness of our crops and the health of our pastures for bountiful herds of goats. Perhaps also, as I write, nightjars will help to tell a useful story. Perhaps one day we may come to find nightjars useful simply through their everyday act of being nightjars, and we may truly recognise our privilege as they connect us to the pristine and the perfect.

*

I once sat below a high, old mountain near the southern tip of Africa, on a foothill covered in low grass. It was a manicured green pasture in a manmade clearing, a green bubble in the middle of a famous forest called Grootvadersbosch. Birdwatchers from all over South Africa and further afield liked to visit this place. Over time the forest had spread out from a crack in the side of the mountain, as if the trees were escaping from inside a great cave. It was on that clear hill in the forest of fleeing trees that I heard my first nightjar and its exuberant song.

Until that evening, nightjars for me had been only words and pictures. My grandfather had talked of them and even mimicked their calls. But on this night the call was a song. And as it sang to me that night, this Fiery-Necked Nightjar, I recalled the description next to a drawing in a book: 'Small to medium-sized, nocturnal and crepuscular birds with small bills, large gapes and eyes, long wings and tails, short legs, cryptic coloration, and comb-like serrations on the claws of the middle toes.'

The description had been as vivid to me as the drawing, each word evoking a picture, until finally a mosaic of little pictures created a bird. I had interrogated each word one by one. To find answers, I had had to read more widely, to learn about other birds in order to learn about nightjars, to enter the world of all birds. 'Crepuscular' taught me about birds that were only active at dawn and dusk. 'Gape' taught me about wide mouths – large enough for goat teats – that trawled and snared like nets in the night sky in a complex mechanism of jaw and skull, like a tightly sprung trap bowed upwards, sideways and outwards. 'Cryptic' taught me about camouflage and mystery, about leaves becoming feathers, sand becoming wings, twigs turning into bones and limbs, and of the obscure blink of eyes on land.

Understanding the nightjar was an initiation into a more refined and sophisticated form of birdwatching; it required watching in a world of darkness. Seeing and being seen at night feed off each other in a coy game of cat and mouse that borders on friendship. There is a kind of theatre in the brush of textures on skin and the hints, glimpses, strange sounds, odd smells, flashes of movement and colours – and oh, the importance of white! Birdwatching by night is a kind of show that always reminds me of the mosaic of little pictures made out of the words in books.

The call of the Fiery-Necked Nightjar is renowned and very much part of the southern African night if you know where to stand, if you know where the edge is, where to prick the bubble. I had always expected to hear it before seeing it. And as I stood there at the beginning of dusk with my friends – I rarely watch birds alone – it was not long before it flew over me. The collage of images leapt off the page and presented itself, complete. And on that clear hill in the forest of Grootvadersbosch the nightjar sang on.

This hill was just one of many hills below many mountains, leading to other mountains and forests (some very remote), and on beyond the forests to the flat lands that led to seas and the edges of the oceans. This hill was the beginning of my night birds. And I determined then that I would see all the nightjars of the world in their many different nights and places.

Seeing the nightjars also meant seeing the birds related to them; birds like the Oilbird and the potoos, birds that were part of the nightjar story, the old story and the new. For to know a bird one should also know its roots, its history. Knowing its past is a preparation for understanding and anticipating its future. The present then becomes a fulcrum balancing the worlds on either side of it, a place to stand and learn. The nightjar and the hill became a point in the present, a point of departure, a road. And as I walked, the road became an ancient path to the first-ever nightjar, past the goat herders at the edges of villages, past the wild forests and the time of our own human beginning. I walked along the path of the primordial, of the ancients before the many extinctions, before spoors became hollows in stone, to the very start of the first path.

Nightjars began as other birds, and these birds began as dinosaurs – all today's birds are modern dinosaurs. To know the nightjar I had to go back to that earlier time, to when scales were feathering into wings, when the sky was softening clouds for flight, when breezes were currents pulling as water pulls fish, lifting life upwards in down-fluff and dandy plumage. It was a time when wide spaces soared and glided in a new partnership; the air newly avian. I imagined an ancient hatching, before the stones of today were fossilised. I imagined the birth of the first nightjar; the birth of the early bird.

Birth from an egg is a solitary affair. When a baby bird cracks its own egg – its bubble – from the inside, and its perfectly shaped shell is rent open forever, it is a lonely moment. Birth from an egg is a struggle, singular and gradual, almost like the unfolding of a shoot from a seed, almost as tight, as quiet, as slow. There is a stirring, a restlessness. First the egg moves, as if what is inside has become too sharp-edged to fit anymore. A tiny, thin fissure appears; a line on the shell, a path... spreading like trees fleeing from a crack in a mountain. The crack becomes more cracks that connect and splinter, freeing bits of shell, until finally, from beneath these bits, lifting and pushing, emerges a bird.

The nightjar egg rocked like a crib. That first reach, that first need to extend a wing to the air, was strong. It was a reach for freedom, an anthropomorphic reach: isolated, delicate and brave. A big head appeared on a long, thin neck in an impossible stretch, and it shuddered, bobbing for air. It was a moment of unyoking, a ceremonial unveiling as its energy uncoiled, all wet and slippery, fresh and wild. Its life was tested; its fitness was perfect. Incrementally and instinctively, the egg had become a bird: nature's variation, nature's choice. In a lengthy succession, generations of bird-like creatures – mutating memories of them – had led to this instant.

During this exquisite narrative of evolution, the story of bird-making, an egg opened one day fifty million years ago, and the bird that unfolded itself was perfectly and uniquely made for the night and its sky, the great ancestor of my Fiery-Necked Nightjar – the Oilbird.

*

To many people a family tree is a chart on a page, a symbol of family to be glanced at for a sense of belonging to the histories and memories of a particular group. It is not a book but a diagram, a connection of names. Yet behind each name, when one studies it more closely, lie stories. And it is only after exploring these individual narratives that one can step back and perceive at last a bigger picture, the fuller breadth and depth of the family landscape. The tree now becomes so much more than a diagram: its branches split from thick to thin, spread and reach for the light, forming leaves, flowers, even roots – the tree lives!

Whatever the pedigree or the lineage, whether of the ancient Chinese philosopher Confucius (the largest recorded family tree), a modern king or a famous scientist like Charles Darwin, a family tree is all about beginnings. A hundred and thirty years after Darwin's death in 1882, his memory is just a small part of a family tree that is still growing and changing, expanding into a wild forest, just like the trees fleeing from a crack in a mountain.

But Darwin is better known for another tree. In 1837 he drew a picture of it in a notebook. It was not a big drawing (the notebook was not very big), just a sketch on a page. This interconnected image of words and graphics was neither writing nor drawing but a hybrid. The annotations were not there to explain the drawing: they were integral to the image, the process, the thinking. This was an idea that needed to be expressed on paper and examined. He must have looked at it, added to it and watched it come about; needed it to come about, to emerge like a mutant. Some lines were thicker where the pen had paused, where more thinking happened; others were light, fast and urgent, ink flowing and changing direction like a journey. Out of the loops, the scratchy lines, the letters, words and sentences, out of the diversity of it all emerged the shape of a tree. It connected his thoughts, his concerns and his answers. It was an evolutionary tree that changed the meaning of family trees forever.

Of this tree, Darwin wrote:

As buds give rise by growth to fresh buds, and these, if vigorous, branch out and overtop on all sides many a feebler branch, so by generation I believe it has been with the great Tree of Life, which fills with its dead and broken branches the crust of the earth, and covers the surface with its ever-branching and beautiful ramifications.[2]

And so it came to pass that all living things were seen to have family trees, and all living things were shown to be of a single tree. This Tree of Life lies at the very core of birdwatching. It is like a map

2 C. Darwin, *The Origin of Species by Means of Natural Selection, or the Preservation of Favoured Races in the Struggle for Life* (6th edn.). London: John Murray, 1872, pp. 104–105.

linking names, both living and dead; it is a route to the past and the future. And at the beginning of the family tree of nightjars – as part of their story and our understanding of them – sits the Oilbird. This bird radiated out across the Northern Hemisphere long ago, sprinkling family memories across the world. It was common then, roaming throughout the darkness, filling the gaps between the stars, linking facts to folklore and the tales of birds on teats.

The Oilbird is still found today in the Neotropics. Edged by the Caribbean Sea and the Andes, the humid world of Venezuela is wild in a mist of rare things. Here forests make clouds intimately and the sky is tactile like breath. Comfort evaporates in a flush of heat as sweat tumbles from one's chin and dribbles across one's skin, running to escape as steam. Cloth sticks constantly and salty shirts feel unnatural; skin is quickly liberated in a kind of yearning for tribal nakedness. The noise of the forest is everywhere: a beetle melody. To inhale is to suck the tastes of fresh earth so sweet that a lush aroma bounces onto your tongue and you swallow sounds in textures. Every leaf strokes you and the caress is damp and soft.

Deep in the forest we walked in a line towards a cliff face that leaned in front of us like a high wall. Trees probed it with fat roots; squeezing and sucking the cracks for food. One swollen tree protruded like a teat, welcoming us tantalisingly and sprinkling shadows about. Like a frozen yawn, a vast cave entrance appeared in the cliff: Cueva del Guácharo. Guácharo was the local name for the Oilbird.

The forest scent grew stronger, and a powerful fruitiness bobbed on the buzz of beetles. Funnelled by the forest, the sound sprayed the smell of flavours onto our cheeks and tongues and clothes, as deliciously familiar as peaches and cream, like pudding, deep, satisfying and soft. Our guide, David Ascanio, smiled; he had been there many times and he knew what we were feeling; he knew the smell. He was one of the great birdwatchers of Venezuela, but he did not keep a list of all the bird species he had seen. It was their calls in the forest that touched him, and he collected their sounds, searching for birds with his microphone. His list was an audible one: he had recorded most of the 1682 species known in his country at that time. He looked at us fondly as he glowed in the heat. He was about to share his country's national treasure.

The unforgettable Willie – one of Ireland's great birdwatchers whom I had just met, and who tragically died on this expedition – bent to pick up a feather. It had the brassy sheen of a trophy, and horizontal stripes in muddy tones with odd forest browns at its edges. Fluffy at one end, and freshly fallen like the new stone chips tumbled from the cliff, its patterns spoke to us as if the night had sent us a gentle message. Today this special feather lies pressed tightly between the pages of my *Birds of Venezuela*, coffined in deep respect as a tribute both to Willie and to the nightjar wing of Nechisar. Whenever I open this book and dream of those forests and their birds, the feather still surprises me as it slips slowly and quietly to the floor, speaking a beautiful name to me: the Oilbird.

David stepped towards the forest cave, and we followed. Slits of stone parted, and an immense hole, shaped like the silhouette of a vast feather, reached up to the sky and down into the land. It was edged in stereotypical stalagmites and stalactites, endlessly dripping new rock.

'No lights please, no flashes,' said David.

Wild places feel wilder in the dark, and we walked into the cave in a tight line. This was a different forest. I was one behind David, third out of ten, and those behind felt like my tail. The ground crunched as we walked between giant rocks, shiny to the touch, cold to the eye, glass-like and possibly dangerous. The cave was cloudless and rainless, although the roof was so high it could have passed for the night sky – and yet it was wet. We followed quietly, still in our thin line of obedience among the stillness. For the things that lived here, it was always night.

David took a few more steps. Sniff-gazing, touch-looking, I began to recognise birds. We were cave birdwatchers at last! All was alive, brushed and stroked into a fresco, a panorama of bird shadows. The whole cave had become birds. Concave and architectural, the walls were also the ceiling, the cave all around us was constructed of nests packed endlessly against each other like the bricks of a catacomb. Each nest was a cantilevered cup of hardened guano, flat and close in a translucent tightness, shivering and fecund in a haze of wings and bodies. It was crowded, yet the little bodies of birds were a vast family: a family tree of fifteen thousand Oilbirds. Each bird had built a structure from its own excrement. Platform after platform had been glued to the rock. Home after home protruded in troglodyte splendour. And every nest was inhabited.

Between one and three eggs were laid in each nest and the chicks grew fast and fat on a diet of forest fruit, until each nestling reached twice the weight of an adult. The name Oilbird arose from the ancient practice of boiling down the fat of these young birds for torch oil. Fattened with fruit, the chicks waddled on ledges, flightless, naked and grotesquely fat, but also beautiful. This was not the lazy fat of indulgence. It was good, instinctive forest fat, baby fat that would one day turn to feathers as time began to trim the birds for the air. Life inside the cave was fat, tropical and excessive, just like the oversized leaves and flowers of the forest.

Oilbirds are unique, not only in their link to nightjars (especially the nightjars of Grootvadersbosch and

Nechisar), but also as the world's only nocturnal fruit-eating birds. Slim and long-winged, they are similar to nightjars but specialist feeders. They never perch in a forest; they only hover, plucking at tropical laurels by night, twisting in a canopy search of remarkable grace. Their large eyes see clearly in the moonlight, guiding them through the branches where voluptuous figs swell, plump pods dangle and oil palms drip fat. Food is rich and plentiful, scattering trails everywhere, like the white dots that pattern the birds' flight feathers, twinkling little braille tales as they flit.

The Oilbirds are completely silent as they fly over the forest, yet inside their cave home they click in the language of bats. We stood and listened to the bounce of their cave talk, felt their trilling voices like the quiver of a shiny beetle's back. The sound was a sculpture. David turned on his head-lamp, and light rubbed the walls of the cave. The Oilbirds stretched, and a greeting hung across that inner sanctum deep in the vast forest – privately, for us.

The smell was heavy and overwhelming. Fermentation bubbles blew up at us from the ground where the nectar had rotted. My feet and my knee-high socks were lost in the sticky, fruity must on the floor of the cave, layered over generations like the rings on a tree-trunk, a calendar of fruit. The cave-floor rustled and crunched with fruit pips, and a large glistening rat scurried away from the noise and the light. Even the birds on the walls were becoming restless as we turned and sifted slowly back to the entrance of the cave.

'We'll wait in the clearing', said David, 'for the start of the evening flight.' We nodded. As I climbed out of the sticky cave floor into the forest freshness, the light felt like cool water, the musty cave air following like a belch.

We spread out and settled on large rocks in the clearing, in a kind of amphitheatre enclosed by the lofty trees and the cliff, whose high walls fashioned a tunnel to the sky, to a high stage on the now silvery clouds. The Cave of the Guacharo was a celebratory place, made for dancing, and I thought of the rum in the nearby village that had been given the same name.

The evening shimmered brightly, and all at once there was puppetry on the dusk. Echoes dangled and danced like mannequins as strings pulled a thousand clicks from deep inside the cave towards us. Then the noise became shadows, and onto the clouds came the birds. Slowly they began, one or two at a time. Then a rush came, blurred like the air from inside the earth; and then a roar like applause, a magnificent drum-roll. Thousands of birds now rushed towards us, to the forest. Some flew high, some very low, and the distance to the clouds was layered in a million laminations of wings. The story of the first nightjar turned like the pages of a book.

*

As continents stretch and lands crack, as oceans become seas and seas become oceans, so the family tree of the Oilbird has gradually evolved, giving rise to new night birds. It is an incremental journey – undetectable before one's eyes, like nightfall – and it continues. It is a story of new islands, new mountains, new forests and new places for life. Descendants of the Oilbirds drifted away from each other and found new places, for there was much space then. They dispersed across the world and diverged from each other, changing elegantly and appropriately, growing like the loops and scratchy lines of the tree in Darwin's notebook. As I followed the history of the nightjars, I read many books, following a story of change, of great differences and also great similarities, of connections and disconnections. It was a distinct and dynamic path that split into many other paths and inhabited many places. Each turn of a page was a long, slow walk, an essential walk that led me from the Oilbird to the potoo.

The potoo sang from the Pantanal, a remote, floodable expanse of forest, the largest tropical wetland in the world and a great refuge of wilderness, of plains and pools. Its heartland lay in Brazil but stretched into Bolivia and Paraguay, beating with birds. It sang cryptically, a silent song that was difficult to see.

I stood in that place with my friends, a small group on a trail made by tapirs. The ground was dry in the prints of ants. We tingled and itched and stung in the heat as our sweat called the mosquitoes like syrup calls bees. The sky was cloudless, the endless blue hovering high above the flatness, impatient as a mosquito. I imagined the smell of jaguar urine lifting as vapour around me. I felt humbled as a privileged visitor, appreciating my temporariness. The land was intolerant of strangers. Only relevant things lived here; each year the waters rose to wash away irrelevance and reward the familiar with greenery and life. It was intensely green: a place of balance between wet and dry and greenness. It was the ultimate wilderness, the ultimate swamp. I stood still as a stick – intent, anticipating, focused – on the edge of the clearing. I was on a path, on an island in the green, on the trail of a potoo, a distant cousin of the nightjar and the Oilbird.

Concentration held everything still, and I truly understood stillness for the first time. Trees are not still, they are stationary. Rocks are not still, they are motionless. Stillness is only the domain of the unstill. Stillness is willed, struck like an elegant stance, powerful, beautiful. It is movement suspended – muscled and charged and pending – like the leap of a frog, bursting with the energy to move, with the knowledge of movement. And that same stillness is the pose of the potoo.

Potoos are solitary and unique to the New World. And they are still. But at dusk the potoos awaken, the dimness of the evening fuelling their movement, unheated but bright in a different way. Now the potoos brush the air in bountiful twirls of moth dust and moth fluff, dipping above the green (a dark, night green) in search of food. They are hunters of insects and feed indulgently on the wing.

But we were standing in daytime. The Brazilian heat loomed over us like boredom – not a cloud in the sky. It was quiet and the heat felt dead. Nothing moved except the wings of parasites. A monotonous buzzing flew in short shadows, bleached in non-colour. We dragged our eyes across the grass and trees, and the green of everything was white like bone. We stood – still again – for the potoo. For it was potoo stillness we had come to see.

Our guide stood at the head of our line, staring. The stare of the birdwatcher is like the stare of a hunter. Then he pointed at a tall tree at the edge of the thicket, a tree with no leaves, no green. '*Obrigado*,' he said to himself quietly and proudly in Portuguese. He looked up into the sky and thanked his ancestors for his good fortune. He had found the bird we had travelled across the world to see; he had killed it with his stare.

We could see only dry branches. Everything was dead. '*Urutau*,' he whispered excitedly in a different language. Glistening with sweat, his fine black moustache bristled and stretched in a proud twitch. As he crouched and peered I walked behind him, staring over his shoulder along his arm outstretched like the barrel of a gun. I imagined being a bullet.

There were no leaves on the tree ahead, but one branch was different. It ended in a swollen blob like a clenched fist. We walked closer and saw the profile of the Great Potoo, perfectly merged with the texture of the tree. Its feathers were bark, without eyes, head, wings, tail or feet. The connection of that bird to its habitat was ultimate. It had become its place, integral, treed and landscaped. The tree and bird defined each other as brown emerged from red and green. I focused my binoculars on a single feather, finely marbled and reticulated, speckled whitish, barred blackish, flecked brownish. Smoothly and gently I followed the surface of the bird and its in-between colour and shape, in between animal and plant. Up the body I climbed with my eyes, up the shape to the top, to the end, where a tiny hooked beak poked the sky, a delicate clue, glinting in victory and success. How beautiful was the harmony of it all. How beautiful the balance: bird and tree, land and water.

From that deep, wild place in Brazil I continued on my travels, finding many more birds of the night in many places around the world, all connected to each other and yet all different. But always it was the nightjars and their like that held the most meaning for me. Owls seemed too accessible, too close, for they are the only night birds of our gardens. To me they were not true birds of the forests – a boyish view that had yet to change. One day I would see them differently, as I had come to see sparrows: everyday yet intrinsic, an essential part of the complete story of the great family tree of birds.

CHAPTER FIVE
TRAVELLING LIKE A BIRD

IT WAS SOMETIME DURING the 1990s when Ian Sinclair pulled open a drawer at the Natural History Museum at Tring. He was doing research for his new book on the birds of the sub-Sahara. There, bagged in transparent plastic, lay a solitary wing, lonely and bodiless, wrapped in mystery. A little dust and dry soil lay at the bottom of the bag, remnants of the land of the wing, sands of a different time. Entombed in the drawer, the wing lay among many other dead birds, skins and discoveries, lacking the grace of a wing in the air. Ian picked it up. It smelled old; it had been in the cupboard for many years. Yet this was a prize, a kind of feathered crown: it belonged to the only bird ever described to science by nothing more than a wing and a few loose tail feathers.

Many years later, Ian at last acquired a detailed description of the site where this lone wing had been found – he received a map. The time had come, he decided. He was determined to seek out the bird. But first he had to assemble a team to accompany him.

Without fellowship there can be no birdwatching; no finding and no seeing. Birdwatching is a shared experience, not only between watcher and bird, but, equally importantly, between watchers; it is here that enquiry becomes debate, that knowledge becomes a place for truth to live.

My telephone rang. It was Ian Sinclair. Would I like to join him on an expedition to find the Nechisar

Nightjar? The name smacked my ear like a dart hitting a bullseye: neat, firm, unbelievable. I had a mental list of the few truly legendary birds that I considered dream-worthy. Ian had just mentioned one by name: the rarest bird on earth! It was a special moment. I plopped into a chair, absorbing his words.

'Yes,' I said.

Two other team members would accompany him on the expedition: Gerry Nicholls from New York and Dennis Weir from Belfast. I was good friends with both of them by then; we had watched birds together all over the world. Each of us would bring different skills to the team, different ways of finding and seeing. But mostly it was our fellowship that Ian was after.

In his famous poem 'Elemental', DH Lawrence writes:

Why don't people leave off being lovable
Or thinking they are lovable, or wanting to be
    lovable,
And be a bit elemental instead?
Since man is made up of the elements
Fire, and rain, and air, and live loam
And none of these is lovable
But elemental,
Man is lop-sided on the side of the angels.
I wish men would get back their balance among

the elements
And be a bit more fiery, as incapable of telling
	lies
As fire is.

Had Lawrence known these birdwatching friends of
mine, I believe he would have approved.

*

I first met Gerry and Dennis in the Venezuelan
rainforest. It was an expedition of incredible intensity
in a place that did not tolerate lies. The great wood
of such a forest can sway and stop the light; in a
click the sun can be gone. Without light, death can
shake the leaves from a beautiful, soft tree – and then,
strangely, one truly sees the tree: its structure, its
hardness, its spikes. The green is gone but life is still
there if you look for it. There is honesty in a forest,
swaying, changing and all-revealing, and you are at
once with DH Lawrence. It was here that I came to
know Dennis, Gerry and Ian, here in the deep dark
of the forest when we lost one of our team members,
suddenly and unexpectedly. He was the best friend
of both Dennis and Ian, and had also become my
friend. We spent weeks together in the rainforest,
adding birds to our lists, finding new blue-eyed frogs
on the forest floor, and following a quiet spoor-line to

friendship, opening up like plants do. Our friendship came initially from a common interest. Birdwatching was our intermediary, our facilitator, and finally our chaperone. Birdwatching created a set of values, a way of looking at the world, a way of walking, talking, thinking, writing and reading. It made a place for friendship to grow.

Dennis was a retired police officer and a man of natural equilibrium. To be a police officer is to walk a moral high ground, a dangerous tightrope above us all. He balanced this life with birdwatching, and was one of the most skilled birdwatchers in the world. That year in Venezuela our birdwatching campfires were particularly dark and quiet: a landscape of honesty without frivolity, our talk intermittent and economical. As we sat at our quiet fires the birds were our stories: we contemplated future bird sightings and discussed the birds in our pasts. At those firesides Dennis taught me how to balance time: time for my birdwatching, and time for my other life of wanting to conserve wild birds.

There is danger in the title 'conservationist'. It can come across as more than a mere act of volunteering: it can be brash, arrogant, pious or condescending. Yet as part of the balancing act, all birdwatchers should want to call themselves conservationists. In this claim lies an unavoidable moment of vanity, but perhaps this can be constructive, allowing for pride, resilience and a strengthening of resolve. Having understood that watching birds also meant watching with friends, for me it also came to mean ensuring that the watching could continue into the future, independently of me but hopefully in a small way because of me, anonymously, yet with an unashamed twinge of self-satisfaction.

'Life is for living,' said Dennis, 'so live life for the birds.' His message was direct, economical and urgent. 'Let the love of finding and watching fuel the conservation.'

Today I smile like a tightrope walker when I go birdwatching. I have come to see that the title 'conservationist' begins as just a label, an expectation, but can embody a journey towards achievement. Being a conservationist-birdwatcher is a romantic notion: I picture Sir David Attenborough deep in a Madagascan rainforest holding up a giant, ancient egg, his famous hands like a cup, his tailored safari shirt clean and unnaturally bright, his eyes keen and watchful. From the romance have come aspiration and ambition, and my label has become relevant as I began to see birds holistically and the meanings of their names became clear.

Dennis is the most physically skilled of all the thousands of birdwatchers I have ever met. He has a way of moving through the undergrowth in silence. The call of a bird and its movement trigger a special type of chase in him. When he locks his eyes onto his prey his head detaches from his body in a way heads are not supposed to. He becomes two parts: a body negotiating and talking to the landscape in delicate, nimble steps, and a head thinking hungrily, still, level and fast as a cheetah. Only once he is with the bird does he become complete again.

I was walking behind Dennis one morning in a leafy Zambian woodland called Miombo by the locals. We were hunting Anchieta's Sunbird – an exquisite, iridescent little bird with sharp wings and a sharp curved beak made for flowers. It was an extremely beautiful bird, at the edge of where beauty becomes brash and vulgar, but it was undeniably beautiful because its colouring was so appropriate – like the rainbow is to rain. It was a small, moving painting: quick, impressionistic and impatiently vivid, shining with the madness of Vincent van Gogh. It was a cold morning, and Dennis took the left flank while I took the right, walking towards the sound of the sunbird in the woodland. Underfoot were layers of brittle, rusty leaves that had fallen in preparation for winter, as if their final task was to keep the earth warm. So noisy were they underfoot that my every footfall triggered arcs of grasshoppers springing. Yet Dennis moved differently. I could see him easily in the hard, glassy air (I could smell him too, for we had been many days in the wilderness), but I could not hear him at all.

'How the hell do you do that?' I asked.

'Walk on the sides of your shoes,' he grinned. 'Roll forward, and use your arms.' Today the leaves underfoot no longer moan at me.

On that same expedition, on a swampy plain further north where Zambia meets the DRC, I dreamed of seeing a Shoebill. The tall, stork-like Shoebill is a unique bird in Africa, heavy and greatly billed, steely grey, and proudly alone. It is a trophy bird for birdwatchers, and seeing it had been a dream since my youth. Dennis shared the same dream. We chartered a tiny plane, a fragile thing without a name, and landed in a clearing in a smelly swamp called Bangweulu – among endless reeds, tight and perpendicular like the bristles of a vast brush. Herds of antelope (Black Lechwe) made the clearing move in endless horns and endless legs.

With a guide who knew the Shoebill and a driver who knew the mud, we set out in an open-topped vehicle to the limit of where the swamp tolerated cars. There we searched out and watched a Shoebill. And what a show bill!

Then Dennis and I whispered a soft curse. Coming slowly towards us was a group of men covered in blood. I could smell the blood – it was new to the sun and too fresh for flies. They came, six men approaching us down the track. Clothed and glistening in blood, their hunched bodies staggered, deformed beneath the weight of carcasses and guns. They were poachers: stealers, killers.

From behind I felt Dennis slowly put his hand on my shoulder. 'Don't look them in the eye.' He had known days like this before. 'Look down and let the driver talk; don't ever meet their eyes.'

I did as he said. For a second or maybe two, I was dead. The act of fear has no time constraints: it can be instantaneous and momentary or last a lifetime. I blinked. Mine was a quick fear.

The six bloodied men spoke to our driver in an incomprehensible language, but their aggression was clear. I stared at my shoes and Dennis stared at his; I could feel his breath on my back as the men spoke over us, their words heavy. Blood trickled onto my shoe from an animal's tongue while I listened hard to the tongues of these men. There were sharp, awkward pauses and repetitions. Some words were slurred, some spat, some short and disobedient. It was unbearably hot and I sensed the men's tiredness. I began to hear stutters and moans. Their language stank of intoxication and blood. The air oozed with marijuana; they were high on it. Their guns were empty and limp. These men had come from far and were beyond more killing. We drove on.

That day Dennis taught me to see fear and remember it. For a birdwatcher, fear can be good, and I drew my strength from the proud, grey steeliness of the Shoebill. Dennis had given me a new meaning for the word 'fear': as something to be used as we use cars, planes and binoculars.

*

I met Gerry on a hot, wet, heavy night in Venezuela. We had just crossed the wide Orinoco River and reached a new town where we hovered in the bright lobby of a newly built hotel. It was a sticky, sweet place that echoed like a fanfare. All was kitschy clean with the stench of oil money, and the brass and polished marble felt like a stage set. There was too much light, and it showed up the cracked plastic trim on the proscenium, the fresh stains on the walls and the beginnings of spider-webs, those shining webs of the forest. Treacly music leaked like oil from a sparkling side-room. We were waiting for an old friend of Ian Sinclair's who had just arrived from New York to join our expedition into the Guianian lowlands.

In burst a little man, hairy and bald, his coloured shirt as bright as the spotlights and rippling with Hollywood razzmatazz.

'Hello, I'm Gerry, but you can call me The Hairy Dwarf.'

We all laughed. Gerry laughed like Falstaff, a cultured, well-travelled, intellectual British laugh (despite living in the US), hearty and sincere.

Gerry shares his laughter readily with birds. The call of some birds can be comic to the ear in a slapstick, anthropomorphic way. Gerry taught me to hear that.

We were back in the rainforest the next day, heading for a tepui: an ancient purple flat-topped mountain that lifts clouds on its back and presses them against the sky. Birdwatching with Gerry is fun and filled with deep meaning. He looks at a bird as a gallery piece – artwork on display – and keeps no list of the birds he has seen. Gerry gathers like a gallerist: he collects visual memories, moments and painted encounters for framing and sharing. He is an immensely skilled birdwatcher whose way of seeing has given much to ornithology.

It was mid-morning as we entered the deep forest, where shadows lost individual shape and became a single shadowiness, far from light, where trees surrender the making of leaves. It was dank and dripping in stems. All the greens were soggy; all was spongy and beautifully quiet. In the quiet green the sun was only a distant dream, an El Dorado trance for a phantom conquistador. Gerry did not know I was watching him as he hung back from the group who had filed along a thin gap. He chose to pause.

He had found a shard of sunshine shaped by the forest that cut a tiny hole in the canopy. Its light was fragile and sharp, stretching up and pulling tightly at the sun. It was tied to a flower, lighting the petals in a glowing red warmth that radiated and bedazzled like the hotel lobby. We watched as a hummingbird came to laugh. Gerry laughed with the bird. We laughed together. The bird buzzed: backwards, upwards, downwards, then forwards, and jerked into a new position on the air. To us it seemed to be having fun. Blurred wingless, its long tail hung like a flying snake – airborne, floating and white in tassels. I laughed again. The bird was a Venezuelan Sylph: a new bird for my list.

Birdwatching has a structure that orders it, much as the structure of a tree trunk with its branches holds the many leaves, flowers and fruits, high fruits and low-hanging fruits. In birdwatching the fundamental structure is the list. In the 'bird list' are the rules of birdwatching, the codes of conduct, one's own private set of rules that are at once universal rules: the rules of honesty, of holding the truth, of what it means to see a bird or to only hear a bird; of what it means to truly watch enquiringly. In the bird list are numbers (for some, unfortunately, it is purely a numbers game) and dates and places, all held together by names, by the titles we give to birds. The list is the place to find all the birds a birdwatcher has ever seen and all the birds a birdwatcher hopes to see. Each list is both a birdwatching past and a birdwatching future. But for me the most important part of the list is the meaning of the names of the birds I have seen. Each name is a story of an interaction, a time of connection with the pristine, a collection of memories, an understanding of our place in the system of natural things, and a hope for the future of that place. And as a tree structure widens in reach, gains an ever-firmer hold on the ground while stretching ever upwards and out to the light, so does the bird list.

My bird list has become a ritual in a process of understanding. Gerry's gift to me, that first morning in the Venezuelan rainforest, was to suggest a new way of seeing. His sylph – the firebird we shared, humming in the forest light, giggling on the light with a playful zip-zap-like Puck – became every bird. And each bird began to offer to my numbers a new theatrical memory, an aesthetic memory and an appreciation for words and stories and connections. In the past, only if asked, I would tell people my number: how many bird species I had on my list, how many I had ticked. It was only a lonely, changing number like a mathematician's problem, reliable and constant. Now it became so much more.

In the forest with Gerry I began to think more deeply – with a depth that comes from being in the dark in daytime – about 'collecting'. I imagined a bird list that would be like owning a zoo, exotic and splendidly diverse without cages. Perhaps zoos tell us about our need to collect from the wilderness.

Today's zoos are institutions for education (and for captive-breeding programmes of endangered species); they are like living natural history museums that grew out of the royal collections of the nineteenth century, the collections of empire. But long before zoos were shaped by communities, the collectors were powerful individuals. No expense was spared; great will was commanded; creatures were hunted, captured, transported and maintained. Around 275 BC, when the teeming city of Alexandria was the largest in the classical world and housed the greatest museum and the greatest library ever known, Egypt's ruler, Ptolemy Philadelphos, called for a menagerie of all wild creatures. And so the library became connected to a living library, and the museum to a living museum. Perhaps that first great zoo was the first great list, the king's list. Perhaps the owning of the creatures, the diversity of it all and the new type of assemblage, the new array, was the beginning of finding our way into nature.

Gerry and I turned to rejoin the line in the forest. The path was only just visible in the tropical language of this place where greens changed: tendrils quickly became trees, and paths wasted no time healing rips and scars in the ephemeral green, saplings stretched back towards the light, glistening leaves flexed and shook off water like tears, fluffy earth mounds expanded and directions evaporated, unpeopled. A single naïve pause could see the forest quickly wipe out any human memory of the place, and one could be lost and slowly absorbed and fed upon.

The group had spotted a bird very high up, and we hurried towards the line. 'Grrraaaaaaaaaaaaaooooooooooooo,' came a call, vast, operatic and powerful, as if the audience was distant. The top of the forest had no acoustic constraints, and I could see every letter of that stretched new word, to which I attached the image of an electric saw. Then there was a flutter of applause and an eruption of splendour. Leaves fell like confetti and tinkled. The air was thick and I could feel the bird ripple dampness downwards: even from such height, mist fell. A shape shuffled with voluptuous arrogance, briefly gripping a spot-lit patch in the sun. It was large and brown with a bald blue-grey head, the Capuchinbird. And I added the sound to the seeing.

*

Birdsong is as synonymous with birds as the cuckoo call is with the cuckoo clock. We come to know birds through the sounds they make. Birdsong helps us to find birds and then see them; it locates them in the landscape in every way. It is a means of communication between bird and bird, between birdwatcher and bird, and between birdwatcher and birdwatcher. Birdsong is a connection. From the Capuchinbird, I learnt that to hear a bird is to see it in a new way. I came to see the sounds they make as the beginnings of their definition, their first contact with the day or night; their finding of the seasons; their way of claiming the wild spaces – or a particular territory. Their linking of sounds became symbols and signs everywhere, and I began to see language, and then many languages. And then I came to see that it was not just birdsong but so much more; that the part that is melodious to our ears – anthropomorphic and pleasant in our world – is just a small part of a complex set of sounds. Bird sounds are as structured as a tree and linked with other sounds – sounds that, if seen from high above, can be seen to shape the landscape of all birds in an interconnecting world of sound: ordering calls, alarm screeches, sounds from wings, from the air, from the water, from above and below – a vast sea of sounds.

Gerry spends his life travelling the world playing music and watching birds, so he understands the structure of music: the layering of sound, modulations, textures, rhythms and tunes (and teamwork).

'A bird makes music,' he said to me in Venezuela. 'How else can you explain such a beautiful song?' He was not considering the science of bird communication and its importance in courting, breeding, sociobiology, territorial definition or any of the various other instinctive and evolutionary processes of bird behaviour. His question was more philosophical, more about us than birds. It was the question of an artist, a musician, containing careful observation of the voice of an animal and finding art in it. It was a question Beethoven had answered in his 6th Symphony, the Pastoral – so rural, so at the edge of where people can go, speaking of walks in the country and the love of wilderness and moving water; music in which the flute becomes a nightingale, the oboe a quail, the clarinet a cuckoo. My own silent response to Gerry's question – to the gift he gave me in Venezuela – was inspiration.

Ian I first knew only through his many books. The day I first met the great Ian Sinclair I was nervous, and also humbled by his presence as part of our team of three. He stood in front of me in the salty mist of the cool sea air on a squeaky beach dune that was bleached, cracked, whalebone-hard and bright white. I was brittle with excitement. Youthful optimism had manufactured a bird for me – a possible new species for Africa! I had been at the spot the previous morning and convinced myself I had found a Cocoi Heron, a South American bird that would have been a new vagrant record for Africa – new for the Africa list.

We stood on the muddy flats at the mouth of the

Olifants River on South Africa's Atlantic coast, a place of sea diamonds and ship skeletons – ships that the sea had stolen. The lazy river couldn't quite push its way into the ocean, and I could hear rough, impatient waves lurking a little way off. The fat-bellied river leaked into the sticky sand, wallowing and quietly estuarine: a lagoon. Everywhere was water, wide and reflective. Hartlaub's Gulls giggled like nervous children at our arrival and prawns zipped into holes like guards on sentry duty.

I pointed out over the shiny surface. 'The bird was feeding out there.' This was my best attempt at a sophisticated ornithological communication. Ian smiled. We started walking and I led the group proudly. At every step, ripples bumped into the sand. I carried my heavy new spotting scope and new tripod over my shoulder, with my new binoculars at my neck. We walked and walked. It was all flat and all new for me. There was no polite talk. We had come here for the bird. It was a serious and important time. It was my first discovery – at last, a contribution to birdwatching history.

Then, with the grace of a seabird, I disappeared. I sank quickly, leaving only a memory on the surface: a bird-fish flutter, a telltale curling of water. Plunging into the pothole was strangely invigorating, momentarily dispelling all social awkwardness. Only on my re-emergence did I feel a lingering sting like that of a jellyfish. My head appeared amid froth and bubbles, and I crawled out with all the finesse of a sea cow. Ian, having avoided the pothole, tugged me out, along with my dripping equipment (fortunately all waterproof). We laughed, though my own laugh was false behind a seaweed-mask of shame.

I disappeared three more times before we found the bird.

Ian took the spotting scope gently and looked at it. He was quiet for a minute. I could feel the quick sun. Everything was at once fast and still and strangely inevitable. He shook his head slowly and looked at me.

'Interesting.' His word was framed in careful encouragement. 'This must be the first record of hybridisation between a purple heron and a grey heron.' At once he dissolved my embarrassment and sheltered me under a clever discovery, a discovery designed by him for me, a trophy of friendship. His was a nurturing answer, a measured response that came of much confidence and considered kindness. That day he became my friend.

We walked back to our car. Gulls called above us again, so white that their breasts were a canvas for everything below, becoming pink and blue as they flew pretty paintings over us. Underwater birds popped to the surface from below – from the potholes – and others floated in a regatta.

'This is only the beginning,' Ian said to me.

✳

Another year I was with Ian in Ghana, a land of cooked, muddled messages. In that squashed little country amid the crowds, modern commerce and ancient cultures, a confusing mixture of protection and destruction prevailed. But there were places where wilderness and wild Ashanti jewels glowed in steam and remoteness. One such precious place was the Kakum Rainforest, a glistening green sanctuary, a vast hothouse of leaves and birds. We had come to see the Grey Parrot – the quintessential parrot of Africa, logo of the pet trade and caged emblem of bird prisons. We had come to see this bird in freedom, owner of its own place and its own language. We had come to find a new symbol for the parrot: unconfined, untouched, unfound.

We dangled forty metres above the forest, swaying in delight on a bridge: a tenuous structure, tensile and tight as a spider web, with many ropes, straight in weight and curled in twists; a world of twine all made from jungle-thread. We moved like a pendulum. It was dangerous, and we became a part of the great roof of trees, insect-like and forested. To be in that canopy was to be leafed and twigged and branched amid the tangible touch of a monster-plant that made me feel beautifully small and dehumanised.

I was part of the treescape, camouflaged in excitement, looking down, not up. Scale and proportion distorted everything. I became big like a flower (or perhaps the flower became small like me). Great big bees buzzed in pollen and probes, and ants made unhurried lines on my skin – almost lazy, almost confiding. I wore a skin of tolerance, intimately. Closeness and textures talked to me in tickles: beetles rested on me; my shoulders became a place on which to mate, and territorial disputes erupted in comical jostles.

We scanned for the parrot, and we listened for it. Ian said we might hear it first because the birds flew in family flocks and called before landing in the treetops. To see a flying Grey Parrot, to find it about the high, wide trees, would be to see liberation, a moment to begin understanding confinement and the world of caged birds (and pets). Birdwatchers look at birds in cages with a certain longing: a longing to see the birds free in their natural place, with natural sounds and colours of wilderness, appropriately as part of a living system, connectors of landscapes and connectors of people to landscapes. For birdwatchers a bird in a cage is not a bird, it is only the sad memory of a bird. It is the polar opposite of birdwatching, at the place of not seeing: the place of objects, of pot plants and chained monkeys; the place of the wingless and the tamed. To not know this is to surrender one's own freedom, to deny one's own place in the landscape, to deny seeing. It is, ultimately, startlingly, to be like the bird in the cage.

Many caged birds have become rare in the wild because they have been removed in unsustainable numbers, in an ironic mass evacuation away from safety. Their beauty – that initial understanding of them in their natural world, with all their sounds and colours and movements; that sight of the very essence of them, that real sighting, that real connection – has been perverted by greed, by the need to possess. The people who first saw them were indeed birdwatchers, but they were birdwatchers who did not linger, did not let the birds pass by them, did not see the rhythms – the need of the birds for the trees and the need of the trees for the birds. They did not watch long enough to see beyond, to the distance, to that which was essential: an intricate, natural system in delicate equilibrium.

We looked down and up and listened to the forest. There were many birds, and it was strange and wonderful to see them so close to us, so anonymous and preoccupied and free. We watched as a green bird gleaned a green berry and squeezed its green juice onto me. A red bird caught a red butterfly while it rested on red. Every colour borrowed colours from others, and cryptic shapes flew and hopped and made the forest move in a gentle rustle, a mingling. A leaf became an insect and an insect a bird. We were all together.

'Malimbe,' Ian whispered and pointed with his nose. Birdwatchers never point with arms or fingers.

Ian has trained his eyes to detect movement and analyse the sound of it instantly: fusing eyes and ears into a single refined instrument of detection. He is a gifted interpreter, able to identify anything that stirs in the deep forest. Like a bright light in the dark, he has worked in every great rainforest on earth; sometimes not seeing the sun for months. He is an old friend of blue shade and black shadow, and he showed me how to sense a bird, how to smell it with the ears.

The malimbe had an incandescent head in a red that glowed in tropical heat: this was the Red-Headed Malimbe. Its body was pure black, like soft, wet bark, and the blackness of the tree hid the bird, detaching its head into a levitating ball of light with a beak. The malimbe was a weaverbird, and it was searching among the creepers for fronds of grass with which to knit. As we watched its search we learnt about leaves and grass as fronds, rope and twine, things other than food, things to work with.

After some time we climbed down to earth. The parrot of our visit had chosen not to arrive, not to see us.

*

One year, Ian and I were on the island of Madagascar, a giant, insular collection of uniqueness. There is no equivalent to Madagascar. It is perfect because it exists without other examples and its creatures are special. It has a finality about it like that of extinction. Most of its birds are found nowhere else, and birdwatchers are called there involuntarily from all over the world. A Madagascan expedition is an obligatory, almost instinctive act for birdwatchers. To travel to places where birds are range-restricted, where the unique is the norm and the pristine becomes a haven, is to embrace the pure. Such rare places structure a global itinerary for birdwatchers. They map the way of comprehending the living world; they are ultimate destinations that lead like a magnet leading a compass.

Trees flushed green and brown, informing and pointing, shook a shaggy welcome on the horizon like a banner at the beginning of a discovery, the beginning of an island adventure. In Madagascar the birds tell the stories of their homes; all is almost a cliché, a living museum.

My first Madagascan dawn was the sound of footsteps running. I was part of the dawn; the running, part of the noise. There was a ripping of clothing, a shredding of skin and a snapping of branches as we followed Moosa, our guide. We were near Ifaty, in the dry south-west, immersed in the Spiny Forest where long leaves pierced, short leaves knifed and fat leaves hooked. The leaves had hardened over evolutionary time: everything was a thorn and all were sharply different.

Deserts are barren heat. Sands hide life and there is stillness to the eye: aridness and sparseness seem amplified in the open sweep of a desert. Deserts are lonely and quiet like hard stone, landscapes of the minimal, treeless in heat. Yet the desert near Ifaty was not like that. It was a forested desert. The earth was like sharp teeth, tight and erect, piercing the ground and the air, squashing space, and all the plants flowed, leafless, into a great nest of bushes. Exquisite baobabs swelled bulbous as fat tails, and we ran. The dryness was silver and valuable.

We were chasing a Long-Tailed Ground Roller – found only in Madagascar, and a potential new bird for my list. It was a bird of the ground, truly terrestrial, owner of the land and the dust, the place of chameleons. Like us it roamed in a gravitational connection, stuck to the planet like a fridge magnet, moving in a slide. The bird was earthed and it was fast, limbed like the wind and quiet on the run.

Moosa had seen one, and the bird had obligingly paused up ahead. The ground roller stood still, its neck stretched high, as if strangely regal and arrogant, its long tail floating parallel to the ground, its length

endless in diversity and complexity. We crouched, and
Ian patted the air, exhorting us to bend lower. And as
we did, light reflected off a wing – the blues of the sea
appeared, a foreign island of blue in the desert, like
the glimmer of the Indian Ocean.

*

Another time Ian and I were at sea, bobbing at the
edge of the continental shelf where Africa bows
towards the South Pole. Here food wells up from
an abyss in the Atlantic Ocean like a larder leaking
herbs upwards towards the sky. It was an intoxicating
place. Albatrosses drifted on the wind and storm-
petrels fluttered above the swell. The water was
rich as syrup, sliding in silvery-golden fish. This was
trawler country, and the fishnets were slippery with
water and fish, calling out to the birds. The surface
of the water became scaled in a frenzy as thousands
of seabirds played and frothed in the waves like
teenagers at a rave. There was a line dance and a ball
dance as birds fed among ropes, on buoys and near
hooks. It was a dangerous time and death happened
there (not only for the fish), but to see this sea was
spectacular. The prize was to see a great seabird, the
Wanderer, king of albatrosses, wings of the ocean.
Within the melee there was always the chance – a
small chance – of a sighting.

Our trawler was wide and Ian stood astern with legs astride, steadied and watching. The ocean was like a jellyfish, translucent and glutinous, wobbling voluptuously in great heaves that reflected the sky in cobalts and purples. We could see onto it but not through it. Underneath swam scary translucent secrets: stings and poisonous things. It was the wild marine, in constant movement, dark and rhythmic like the night, vast and rhythmic like the days, repetitive and heaving, up and down and up again, yet oddly terrestrial in shape. I breathed in the spray like dust and licked a crust of salt off my lips.

A wave bowed down, sucking the horizon with it, and a bird appeared. It did not bother to fly because it did not have too. It owned the place like a parrot might own a tree. It commanded the sea royally to hold it in the air. It skated above the cold water, graceful as an ice dancer. It was hunched in Antarctic white, its wings stretched from north to south.

'Wanderer to starboard!' Ian shouted. 'Flying left to right, forty-five metres out, behind the gannets.' And he smiled.

One of the great sophistications of birdwatching lies in being able to quickly tell others where a bird is, and Ian was the master teller. This gratifying skill of 'getting onto the bird' is a revered etiquette that requires calm eloquence and takes considerable time to learn. Ian has spent many years teaching me this polite and necessary skill. I enjoyed getting onto that albatross.

Each new bird was a number, each number a name, a title, and a story of friendship and understanding. My friendships were an internship in the pristine, and birdwatching the great provocateur.

And then, quite suddenly, the four of us coalesced into the Sinclair Expedition of 2009.

CHAPTER SIX
EYE OF SOLALA

WE FOUND AN OLD LINE in the earth on the plain at Nechisar. It was a tired track, a spoor of clay and infrequent wheels, where mud had hardened into rough pockmarks, bumpy like braille. We imagined those wheels of twenty years ago, the wheels of discovery. We imagined the wing, squashed and preciously preserved, a softly dusted and unpolished wing, a wing badge of the birdwatcher. And we dared to imagine the glory, the fame, of finding the rarest bird on earth. We imagined and waited. And that evening our imagination took new flight. We had found the site of the wing.

We stood on it, stamped it onto our minds just as surely as it had been stamped into that red earth: an embossed sign of immense importance to science, and a lonely invitation from nature to birdwatchers. We were characters in a boyhood adventure story, and we followed the X on our map to the best place to wait, poised like the potoo for nightfall.

Bhanti, our guard, climbed out first, his ancient rifle protruding reliably. Then we too stepped out into the profound silence of the plain – lion territory. Bhanti gazed across the grass; he had the mane of a lion about him, the fur and the knowledge of a lion. We stretched our limbs for the first time in many hours. My knee clicked refreshingly, and I walked down the track into the silence. I wanted to be alone in this silence after the noise of the car. I needed to feel the wide, quiet air moving freely against my face in the softness of the warm evening. Silence wrapped me like a blanket, touching my cheeks snugly. I pulled the silence towards me with open hands and imagined the wing again.

Silence is close to stillness: a companion in birdwatching, and also a skill. Silence is a virtue, an opportunity to contemplate and to enjoy quietness. It is also a place in nature owned by the beautiful sounds of birds. And I stepped further into that silence.

'What goes up must come down...' shouted Gerry, face contorted skywards, binoculars balanced on his large nose as he walked and talked while staring into the heavens.

'You watching clouds now?' I asked.

He smiled sardonically and pointed at a white wisp high above. Then I saw it, a dot ascending in perpendicular flight.

'A lark,' we both said.

'Flappet Lark,' said Ian.

The sky was turning to evening in a graceful swirl of luxuriant, iridescent lilac hues, swelling in magical luminosity against the puffy white clouds. The bird pulled these new colours earthwards like a waterfall of tinted inks in the glowing satin of dusk. It descended slowly in winged tension, growing bigger and still bigger. Suddenly feathers exploded, a punch struck a little hole above us, and the bird was gone, its song ended. As a lonely feather twirled slowly down in the slapstick humour of an animated cartoon, the dark silhouette of the lark flew sideways, dead and low in the talons of an African Hobby. As the falcon beat heavily towards the mountains and became part of them, stillness returned to the plain again. I mourned the lark, although there was a strange beauty in its death: in the suddenness, the finality, and the lingering hymn of its movement. And as we said goodbye to the lark and to the sun, I was left with a new word: larkless.

'Death is natural' was a cliché I had heard in many sermons of advice at school, a great intangible religious concept to a sheltered youth like me. I never understood the words until I watched the lark fly in that exquisite sky. Its death was black, quick and merciless, yet also colourful and appropriate, shining with interconnectedness. One day, I thought, I want to die like the lark, and fly onwards differently.

Beside me, Bhanti spoke. I looked more closely at his machine gun. It was old and a little dented; it had clearly been used many times. His eyes became falcon eyes, eyes for hunting larks. He pointed ahead and whispered in a language I did not know.

'Gobeze,' I asked, 'what is he saying?

Gobeze smiled. 'He says cattle are coming.'

Africa is resilient in its remote, scattered paradises. It has given new life and also hidden life. The plains where we now stood were paradise for birdwatching. I was in a hidden Africa now – an often dangerously romanticised Africa – where forests are too vast and thick; mountains too high and distant; valleys inaccessible and plains forgotten. But Bhanti reminded me that Africa is also a land of flesh: the flesh of fellow tribes traded across oceans, rivers of flesh bleeding in traitorous brotherhoods; raped flesh turning soils red in a sea of violation; white flesh scouring great holes; land deepened and never quite green again; untamed flesh embattled, rotting on plains, displaced and fleeing.

Then the cattle came. The distance shivered in dust and a stirring thing puffed, hovering patiently just above the grass. A mist of earth was momentarily sent into the air, orphaned. Shifting cattle wrestled to claim a place on the horizon, a living edge to the sunset, a blurred fracture of the pristine, breaking my hope of sanctuary. The plain became peopled in cattle. Grass broke with loud cracks in the silence as the cattle began to move towards us. The wild eland spoor at our feet was undone, trampled into a scar. We were on a cattle path now, a path of many cows.

A bird settled on a cow and I started to look at the cows differently – not because the bird had landed (wild, brown and medium-sized but too distant to identify) – but because of the way it landed: the familiarity, the nonchalance, the cow's acceptance of it. A bird may land in many ways: like a plane stopping at the end of a long flight path; in the slow, gentle drift of a ship; an enquiring docking for shelter from a storm; in a settling for the night; an alighting on a nest; a frantic, urgent dive for cover; a swoop for prey; a stoop. Landings can tell a birdwatcher many things, and in all my watching of birds it is always a singular moment of enlightenment: that final transition from air to land, that instant in which I read the mood of the bird.

This wild, medium-sized brown bird had landed delicately, and the cow's wild dik-dik fur had twitched in acknowledgement. The bird's claws and feet appeared adapted to the skin of the cow and the shape of its back, and as the cow walked and fed, so too the bird walked and fed. It appeared to pull insects off the cow: cow-irritating insects obviously of great nourishment to the bird. The bird and the cow needed each other. Earlier that day I had seen such a bird on an eland – the largest antelope of Africa – and it too had walked with the eland.

Looking at the great herd of cows, I no longer saw dust; I saw cryptic, coppery and appropriate colours, shades blended to match the landscape, tails mingling and flicking rhythmically. And in between the cattle, swaying like tails, walked men with long spears. These were not just domestic cows; they were tribal cows, Guji cattle. I watched another bird land on a different cow.

Environmental conservation is a complex concept in Africa, and it belongs, in part, to the story of the cows. Conservation cannot survive as an idea imposed, as a directive packaged in smiles of international aid (laced so often with condescension). It cannot exist in remote and abstract concepts of science and biodiversity. It cannot exist detached and disconnected from the people of the place to be conserved. As I watched the gathering of cows and sharp, tall men, I listened again to the silence: cattle and men talked; the cattle talked like eland and so did the men; men herded cattle and cattle herded men; the memory of antelope on the plains endured in the shape of cattle, as men endured and so did the plain. I watched the birds land. On this very edge of the cultivated and farmed, on the edge of our human world, at the furthest places humans occupy, people are a part of the pristine. It is a precious place, and it is rare. And I smiled at this herd of cattle and men and birds.

*

The mountains of the Nechisar Plains define Nechisar like a frame defining a painting. Without that range of bulging hills there could be no plains. The Amaro Mountains gave an edge to my view, they made it complete. And as I looked down closely at the texture of the ground, sprinkled evenly in coarse grass, soft soil and volcanic pebbles, I was reminded again of the wing, of where we now were and why we had come.

We had reached the end of our two-day trek, and we stood at dusk on the discovery site of the rarest bird on earth. We had been meticulous in every step of our plan.

Ian had spent a long while working on a special lamp, in a language of curses and spanners and other tools I did not recognise. It was a nightjar-capturing lamp, he said, which he had made with great success many times before. The technique was to create a fiercely bright lamp attached to the car battery with a very long strand of flex, allowing the holder to creep right up to the nightjar while maintaining the light at a constant intensity, so that the bird, stunned by the light, could be handled with ease. The prize would then be viewed, photographed and hastily released back into the night, unharmed.

'Guys,' Ian said now with a note of melancholy, 'we're unlikely to find any nightjars with all these cows coming down the track.'

But we were here now. There was no giving up. So, holding our stillness with all the patience of the potoo, we waited for the darkness. When at last it came, we flicked the switch on the big, black spotlight.

There was a pop. But no light appeared. Our only bulb had blown.

Not only were we to share the evening with a noisy herd of cows, but we now had to abandon our primary bird-catching strategy.

A little dust kicked a breeze into the air. I spat out the dust and looked across to the mountains again. I found them oddly calming, their wiggly edge like a child's crayon-drawing of water. The largest, closest mountain was rounded like a cranium, sprouting a small forest on top like a tightly combed fringe.

'Quiet!' urged Ian suddenly. 'A Donaldson-Smith's.'

And so began our nightjar night.

We climbed into the car and Gobeze started the engine. Our only option was to drive very slowly, scanning the evening with the small spotlight connected to the cigarette-lighter socket. This kind of spotlight has a very short cord, and can only be used from within the vehicle. Our only chance of a nightjar capture now was to catch a bird in the headlights on the track ahead. Birds seen from the side-windows could only be studied through binoculars: my spotlight would be enough for identification but unlikely to mesmerise it for capture.

Hunting with spotlights is a thrilling way to find and watch birds. There is something especially exciting about hunting at night. It is a concentrated experience: focused, intense, strangely fundamental. But 'hunting' is an uncomfortable word for birdwatchers. They may chase birds or look for them, but they do not want to own the act of hunting. Yet to deny this is to miss an important connection, a feeling as strong and intrinsic as the need to eat. Hunting in birdwatching has nothing to do with killing, but everything to do with an ancient, powerful and fulfilling way of seeing. Hunting in birdwatching allows one to glimpse momentarily through the eye of the eagle.

Birdwatching expeditions at night are always wild in creatures – often new kinds of creatures – and at once familiar in our undeniable urge to hunt. My first spot-lit hunt was on my uncle Tykie's farm in South Africa when my brother Arch and I were just eight and nine. Uncle Tykie drove us in a car without a roof. It was a savannah night spiked with branches. Vicious leaves and thorns whipped about, lancing our little faces in giant pricks, dangerous for little boys. Scatterings of forest were patchy on the big dark plain. The night twinkled with discovery as my brother and I giggled in exuberance, our cheeks stinging with scratches and exhilaration. Uncle Tykie was a great hunter of Africa. Beside him sat my aunt Vladi and my mom – a birdwatcher – while my brother and I held the spotlights for the first time, hunting for springhares.

'Got one,' I yelped, locking my beam onto a furry little animal leaping along the track in front of us.

My uncle shouted an instruction to my brother, who leapt out and ran confidently. The springhare bounded along, spot-lit like a performing acrobat, a kind of hopping rat, half kangaroo, half mouse, lunging into the sky in fantastic loops. I stared at its little body, its exaggerated legs and its long tail following behind cooperatively. My brother was to chase and catch the rodent by its tail. He dived bravely and dust sprang up, but the springhare disappeared untouched. We all laughed, and I was filled with love for the springhare and for my brother, uncle, aunt and mother.

A childhood hunt is a quite exceptional gift to a child. It is an anointing, an awakening of an ancient memory: the uninhibited splendour of instinct revisited. Hunting must be recognised and celebrated in the context of one's love for the natural world. My uncle gave me the gift of hunting: of seeing enquiringly. He reminded me of an old pleasure, of its intimate role in the workings of wilderness. And I began to hunt birds.

Hunting is necessary if one is to collect, for collections come from hunting. And on this night the Nechisar Plains were our hunting ground.

A Kori Bustard rocked through the evening grasses on its last hunt of the day, the white flecks in its huge, closed wings glowing in the sunset. 'The heaviest flying bird on earth,' Gerry adopted the disconnected voice of a wildlife documentary, 'heavier even than the Mute Swan or the pelicans.' These words were not the words of a hunter, not derived from watching and truly seeing. Gerry was perfectly aware that we knew all this; he was merely reminding us to watch like birdwatchers. The Kori Bustard seemed wingless, undecided about flight. We imagined it would soon sink to the ground and sleep, dreaming of being truly terrestrial like the ostrich, or truly aerial like the swift. Other animals were asleep now.

Then our lights picked up eyeshine.

Eyeshine has a clear scientific explanation based on lenses, prisms, refraction and reflection, interesting in itself as a mathematical calculation. But eyeshine for me is a different experience: it is a gemstone borrowing the light; it is the unpredictability of light, the ricochet, the sparkle, the energy – free yet trapped – sometimes red, sometimes green and sometimes a yellow-white. I see a winged gemstone, a precious living thing. I see a white night-flower, bright and hovering in the moonshine, its green attachment hidden in the dark; or an iceberg floating on a huge ocean near a ship; or a lonely candle on a desk on that ship – images that glow mysteriously, beautifully, each one a part of bigger things, of untold stories. The flower belongs to a thin, tall stem that makes it whole, the ice hints at a mountain upside down, the flame is a flag for the wax and a light for writing. All are signals, signs, hints that represent the hidden.

The night seems to own the eyeshine, releasing

only chosen views after careful negotiations with the torch. Our view was quickly channelled, captured by distant sounds released like lyrics in verses. Unlike the dawn choir of the forests like those at Lake Langano, the call of the evening was an ensemble of solos on scattered stages across the plain. There were distant screeches; there were also flatulent murmurs at our feet – perhaps the burps of toads emerging from holes dissatisfied at the closeness of our wheels. Any new sound that claimed airtime was important. Unlike radio or television airtime, this was a living time with a fresh, purely wild meaning infinitely removed from the workings of machinery; the feral selection of sounds on the wild air.

We did not know the call of the Nechisar Nightjar. Nobody did, so all sounds were potential clues of discovery. We knew the calls of all other known species of nightjars, and the repertoire of Africa's nightjars presented considerable diversity: some like barking dogs, others like crickets, some varied and melodious like robins, and some even as flatulent as frogs. We listened with our eyes too. That night I learnt how eye-listening in the darkness focuses the mind. Every sound was answered by a flurry of searching beams, sharp rods of light cutting, chopping and jerking, followed by a muffled commentary, mainly from Gerry.

A herd of antelope grunted softly in the detached way one may mumble while dreaming, a contact call to another world in the night. Because the antelope were pale like cows, the moon helped us see them. Our wheels crackled and turned slowly. A fertile sky of insects hummed, tiny bodies glistening in a sort of comet fire, streaking everywhere, shooting off into oblivion in a universe of flashes, some crashing and frying against the car lights. I smelt their sweet smoke and remembered their flavours as they struck the car and stuck. This was nightjar air.

What a beautiful moment it was to witness Ethiopia opening privately, reminding me of the generousness of my adventure. Pure night became even more extraordinary and the pure wildness of the night was exquisite and abundant. We were in the embrace of one of the most remote places on the planet: a world of complete nature. So much of what was before us was new to science, and also new to the lists of my collections, my memories. I looked at my friends and their silence smiled. And together we searched for the rarest bird on earth.

'Nightjar!' said Dennis.

'Stop!' said Ian.

I hung from the side-window (yet again). Dennis held a bird illuminated in his light, squashed like the many volcanic rocks of the plain, like a frog. All was pebbled and stoned and quiet and vivid. All was still. All eyes glinted, mesmerised. The bird was distant: a half-wink of eyeshine. Ian and I focused our binoculars instinctively, and instinctively the bird flew, perfectly lit as it lifted and wobbled and reflected. Emotions stung all over me – inside and on my skin. Never before had I enjoyed such exhilaration. Never before had I felt more connected to the pulse of life.

'That's it! That's the bloody bird!' said Ian.

I had hoped to hear him say that; I had prepared for it. He had not really expected to see this bird. From twenty years of past experience in Africa, his expectations were half-expectations, half-hopes. But that half-hope had brought him here – and the rest of us had followed – all the way to these plains.

He watched the giant wings rising upwards. I flew up to be with the bird, possessing it in an air of partnership, talking to it like a friend. I climbed with the bird into higher air, private air. We glanced below at the car like a little ship, squatting solidly, grey and foreign, bursting with torch-light flickers: little twitching candle flames. And I watched myself down there with my fellow birdwatchers, all looking up into the stars. I could see myself smile, and feel the glow. I became different. The buoyancy of wings was everywhere, padding my mind as the bird and I floated together, bobbing about.

Bright in Dennis's light, the bird climbed gently again, this time without me, alone. Dennis's beam guided it higher and the nightjar flapped like a giant moth. Feathers exposed everything honestly; the stars made a powdered shine around our bird. There was glamour in its form; the famous wings open.

There was a sudden shift in mood. Discovery changed to science: melodies turned to sonographs; the grace of a dance turned to anatomical detachment; a sculpture carved itself into a bird. The Nechisar Nightjar named itself for us that night. All we had to do was look and list (and write). The cold rules of identification dictated our way. Knowledge of the structural characters that made up the bird demanded visual recognition, and like soldiers in formation we marched from fact to fact, ticking: shape of feather; colour of feather; length of feather; movement of feather; angle of feather; arrangement of feathers; patterns made in feathered relationships.

Then it was gone. The immediateness of its departure was as shocking as its arrival. I looked down at my watch. All seemed new as my watch ticked. The time was half past seven in the evening. I had been with the bird for six seconds, the most exciting six seconds of a lifetime.

The experience of wilderness is very personal: the one-on-oneness, feeling part of a chain reaction that seems to link all things, one to the other, like falling dominoes; the utter dependence of one creature on another; the tremendous privilege of sharing a wild secret, an interaction, so intensely present and important. This experience was also very private and rare. We were the first birdwatchers to ever see a Nechisar Nightjar: the only living bird ever described scientifically yet never seen by science; never seen by anyone who was not a part of its world; never watched enquiringly. A mystery had quite literally been solved. Fiction had emerged as fact. A myth had flown into the air that night and turned into truth. It was a bird that ticked every cliché in the book! A whispered dream of a bird shouted across the world. It was a vital shout: a wing that had claimed itself as a resurrected creature, whole, complete and alive; a sign to our civilised world that all was not tamed, a reminder that nature's mysteries were resilient and strong. From time to time the undiscovered is discovered, and at those moments a call is sent out from the untamed, a reminder to us – the tamed – that all is not owned by us. Sensitive places on earth still hide and protect, waiting to overcome the insistent occupation of the civilised. I thought of the tall penguin leaning alone into winter, tipping forward against the endless cold and endless wind, persistent and confident of a spring hatching and a spring victory. Nature can talk in determined tones and send the occasional message of survival.

Holding my torch tight in my teeth, I bent to scribble in my little black Moleskine notebook, where I always record my meandering observations and thoughts – sometimes frivolous – about creatures and strange places; memories and names and words that become reference files stacked high on my shelves back home. Aware of the importance of the moment that night, I wrote with responsibility, and my book became suddenly heavy and hard, legal and declaratory, serious as a headline. The words came slowly, letter by letter, considered and daunting to write. I described everything I could about the bird, particularly its large size and its huge and distinctively bright white patch at the base of the carpal joint where the primary feathers affixed to the wing. So distinctive was this feature that I recorded it as diagnostic and definitive, almost 'skua-like' in form, I wrote, capturing Ian's words exactly. I also carefully noted the time, weather conditions and flight pattern.

Then the car began to move again as we hunted for a second sighting.

Birdwatching is often about glimpses, flashing clues of identification rationed to extremely condensed moments of verification: the plop and ripple on a still pond that confirm the crocodile eyes; the flick of black ear-tips in long grass in the smell of lions. Birdwatchers are trained to find certainty in seconds. The luxurious pose of a bird resting on a branch is the easy, often self-indulgent, sighting. The challenge of a blur dropping against a textured cliff, crying in the cryptic scream of an unknown falcon is a more difficult sighting, perhaps more satisfying, and naming is quicker. Sometimes birds do not come to us easily; we need to go to them, enter their place, learn of them by becoming a part of that place, a place that often rewards patience, even if the visit exists only between a blink and a breath. The wonderful act of birdwatching is a complete escape from one place into another, and it is made of non-time in a quintessence of feathers.

Then it was time to head back to our 'camp', our base in the village of Arba Minch. An expedition would be incomplete without a 'camp' – the cliché was appropriate. It would take us the rest of the night to reach the village, and as Ian signalled to Gobeze, I adjusted my imaginary pith helmet, preparing to leave the plain. I switched off my spotlight. We would have to return the following night with new equipment better suited to getting closer to the nightjar, better suited to a capture or for taking photographs.

Silence slipped over the car. The dark slid down the windows, over the seats and over the clichés, and we became singular in a lonely hole far away: a quiet box for thinking. Contemplation came clearly; the closest I had ever come to myself. At times happiness is intensely private: a place of solitude and yet immense abundance.

Knowing now that the bird did indeed exist – alive – we began to think about telling the birdwatching world. For in birdwatching, 'proof' is a big, complicated word.

CHAPTER SEVEN
ANIMALCULES AND
EVERYWHERENESS

LOOKING UPON A LIVING thing in nature that has never been seen by science before – looking closely and with intent – is a moment filled with many feelings. It is a moment of enlightenment; a reminder that wilderness is still filled with secrets. It is exhilarating in discovery. It is exciting because of its mystery – the beginning of new questions. It is wildly satisfying instinctively. It is the domain of those who watch nature enquiringly. Links are made, problems resolved and evolution reigns in loud affirmation. It is also a comforting moment, when old laws are strengthened and the rules of our world make sense.

Today more than ever we recognise diversity, ancestry and lineage. It is time for clarity. It is time for the unconquered creatures (the unnamed ones) to surrender feral truths in a grand, slow, stooping bow. By the simple act of watching, the undiscovered becomes discovered, the untamed is tamed. Perhaps it is a sad time; a reminder of our shrinking world: an unveiling of the innocent; a betrayal of the free – like the caging of a parrot. Perhaps it is the beginning of the end, the final pages in the story of us. Or maybe it is a sign that we are at last learning of our origins and our future, a warning that there is little time left, that our destination is death – we are running out of space and the stench of extinction is massing on the horizon. And so discovering life that is unknown to science and to our world reveals a human need: the deep need to name so that we can learn.

We name our homes, streets, suburbs, cities, nations and continents; we name the stars and beyond. We name ourselves, our possessions and our every view. We name the animate and the inanimate. Naming is how we find our way through the physical landscape and the landscape of the mind; it is how we describe our existence. And on our journey to describe our world, we embrace wildness as the only way to get close to it, and we are enriched in the act of naming.

The natural and the unnatural define each other, and they define us, like the sea defines the land, like the mountain edge defines the sky, like a flower defines the soil and a humming bird defines a flower in a rainforest clearing. As we continue to watch creatures and their interactions in the living assemblage, the unnamed become named, and the sophistication of naming serves to humanise nature, turning it perhaps to non-nature.

In the words of the famous watcher of ants and father of sociobiology, Edward O Wilson: 'Nature is that part of the original environment and its life forms that remains after the human impact. Nature is all on planet Earth that has no need of us and can stand alone.'[3]

---

3 E.O. Wilson, *The Creation: An Appeal to Save Life on Earth*. W.W. Norton, 2006, p 15.

Those of us who sail the pristine admit a powerful relationship. Ours is a titillating gaze. Marcel Proust suggested that 'the real voyage of discovery consists not in seeking new landscapes but in having new eyes'.[4] To stand in a meadow on a rolling plain and watch a flower open for the first time is to witness a revelation – petals describing a unique type of living thing – but it is meaningless to us without a name. Science has shown us how to name, and we find security and satisfaction in its systematic ordering. Science illuminates the living with its great clarity, describing organisms, defining boundaries and banishing chaos to reveal our earth as a bright biosphere of life.

We have always named. Since we first walked upright, away from the trees and into the open on the ancient rolling plains of Africa – just as we began to become people – we named. After a great time, Aristotle separated the most noticeable of living things into the 'blooded' and the 'bloodless'. In the Middle Ages, experts created alphabetical dictionaries – herbals – that classified and described the medicinal plants. Books were made, arranging these labels into sets and subsets. Then in the mid-eighteenth century, Carolus Linnaeus founded our modern system of scientific naming. As scientists compared and further classified living forms, the Linnaean system of

---

4 J. Griffiths, *Wild: An Elemental Journey*. Hamish Hamilton, 2007.

binomial nomenclature was arranged into species, genera, families, orders, classes, phyla and kingdoms. Today this form represents our best understanding of evolutionary relationships. Within larger orders such as songbirds, still more layers of classification have been needed to tell the story of evolution, such as parvorder, superfamily, sub-family and tribe. This systematic method of discovering, describing, arranging and listing is called taxonomy, from the Greek *taxis* (to arrange) and *nomos* (law). And so we continue to name.

Science searches out nature's laws as children seek nurturing. Science is disciplined and obedient, always guided and comforted by the laws of the wilderness. Yet of the all the different species of living organisms on earth, so far only one and a half million are known, described and formally named. Studious and academic taxonomists claim that there are ten million other species alive today; some even put the number at fifty million or more. The total number of species that have ever lived on earth has been estimated at between seventeen million and four billion – a disquietingly vast and vague range.

To be named and listed is to be represented in the ordered mind of science. A label is stamped like a signpost for scientific query and navigation, a marker on our human map of the natural, a civil flag on a feral chart. In a string of words, we define for ourselves and our world an image of each type of living thing: we visualise a tree, tall, hard-stemmed and upright with leaves; or a fish, wet, scaled and watery-tailed; or a bird, feathered. The vagaries of a general view of wilderness leave us unfulfilled; we have a need for more detail, for the specific. To satisfy our unique way of seeing, the tree, the fish and the bird must become named.

On the Nechisar Plains we witnessed the naming of a bird. Rather suddenly, the bird in our mind became a night bird, then a nightjar, then the Nechisar Nightjar, *Caprimulgus solala*. And a list began to form. Science places nightjars into a group – an order – of birds called Caprimulgiformes, composed in turn of families: the nightjars (Caprimulgidae), the potoos (Nyctibiidae), the Oilbird (Steatornithidae), the frogmouths (Podargidae), the eared nightjars (Eurostopodidae). This system of intellectual order and understanding allows our minds to interpret existence. This is the beautiful world of naming, and this is where birdwatchers live with their lists. So the definition of a 'species' lives as a taxonomic rank for us, as a unit of convenience that arranges the wilderness for us, helping us to configure and understand it. The naming of species allows for measuring, for testing, and for looking upon the vast diversity of life. The identifying of species helps us to theorise and learn. Species comprise all of known life and all of our living reality.

Yet as birdwatchers talk around their firesides, a niggling question often recurs: What is a species? Profound discussions about what does – and should – define species have taken place at firesides for a very long time. Among the collectors and inquisitors of life these rich discussions sometimes flicker unpredictably, casting shadows of doubt, flaring occasionally into frustration and disagreement.

When a wild population is separated from another wild population so that they no longer transfer genetic information between them, something special happens. As the specific conditions of a locality continue to influence reproductive success, certain gene variants become more – or less – common among the population. Nature shapes life powerfully and surely, determining and selecting, sculpting environmentally and moulding evolutionarily. As the heritable is embodied in the living, new forms grow and manifest new life, and after a time, isolated populations evolve genetic differences from others. And so a new species is born that requires a new name. Sometimes the genes drift, inheritance is influenced by chance, and a random message prevails like a gust of wind sweeping a bird left instead of right, so beautifully biochemical, biological and biodiverse.

Ernst Mayr, the famous evolutionary biologist and ornithologist, defined a species as 'a group of actually or potentially interbreeding natural populations, which are reproductively isolated from other such groups'. He proposed that speciation – the act of creating a new species – occurs when a population no longer breeds with another population. It has then become a separate evolutionary entity, a named species. This is the Biological Species Concept. But a question has been asked that this concept cannot answer: How can we define species on the basis of sex if species never come into contact with each other?

Some say that Africa's northern White-Faced Scops-Owl and its southern White-Faced Scops-Owl are two separate species. They look similar but exist separately, both perfectly adapted to their similarly hot, arid, thorny-treed nights on the savannah. Both have been moulded by their landscapes, but as they move and bob, their shapes mirror each other, their sounds echo each other, speaking of a common history. Yet they are different and physically distant, separated by vast forests, plains, mountains and time. Africa has stretched between them, walling them from each other naturally. The poet might wonder if they have some ancestral memory, some lingering longing for each other; the scientist might question whether they have a genetic memory of each other.

Are they one species or two? How will we ever know? How do we measure objectively in this naming? We cannot sit and watch for mating; there will be no interbreeding here to confirm a name. We must turn to a new way, find a new rule so that we can sit comfortably again with our world reordered, our humanity made safe again in the feral.

And what if, as time reshapes the wilderness, two species once separated should meet and interbreed? Are they one species again? Were they one species all along? The Biological Species Concept would say they are. But perhaps they are not.

Three different species of southern African bulbul – the Cape Bulbul, the Red-Eyed Bulbul and the Dark-Capped Bulbul – appear very different to the birdwatcher's eye, and we label them contentedly and surely. They live in three bio-geographical areas that are environmentally different, yet breed with each other along a contact zone. Why then do we call them different names? Curiously, however, hybridisation is not reconfiguring the three populations into one; in fact, time appears to be reinforcing the species boundary. Here the act of sex fails to define these species because they remain different despite interbreeding.

Some birds that inhabit an unclear, in-between place remain unnamed. Are they the new birds of an ephemeral wilderness, a non-species in an unsettled landscape? Are we witnessing speciation in process, or merely the strengthening of existing definitions of species in a stable existence? Or is it time to look past the act of sex for a new rule of what a species is?

Many species are widespread. We often see the same species across continents and oceans, following the earth as it curves and bends into a giant ball of life. Although wilderness sprinkles a living diversity over the global surface, with many isolated, localised and even rare forms of life, we also marvel at species that are highly successful, common and abundant. One such species is the Greenish Warbler.

The Greenish Warbler – a little grey-green bird of the leaves – has a special story to tell about the meaning of species and speciation. It appears to have originated on the southern rim of the famous Himalaya Mountains. Over much evolutionary time the population spread out to the east and west, as if the great mass of mountain had interrupted their northward journey. And so two populations diverged and bent in slowly moving arcs towards the north. They spread incrementally as a light cloud floating above us becomes a dark cloud far away. And as they moved their green colours changed, their songs changed. We watched and then we changed names. As the populations moved further northwards, around the mountains, they finally met again as strangers, with extreme variations that met the test of distinct species (for us). But these extremes were linked by intermediates.

In the science of ornithology, this group of warblers is regarded as a classic example of a 'ring species'. They are extremes of a continuum. They are a connected series of neighbouring populations – of neighbouring colours and sounds – that can interbreed with relatively closely related populations, but for which there exist at least two end-populations in the series that are too distantly related to interbreed. These populations and their interconnectedness are an example – in our living time – of speciation. They are a testament to genetic divergence, and they tell us what a species is and how it can emerge. As we travel the journey of their distribution in a colossal loop around the mountains, we see a visual story of gradual transformation. With every incremental variation in plumage hue, we see evolution colouring the change.

In watching birds such as owls, bulbuls and warblers, we are always searching for the definition of 'species'. Sex has helped us but it has also created uncertainty, so we look for other clues to help layer our answers more rigorously, to check and cross-check. We look past visual similarities in physical form, past the blurred world of interbreeding and the act of sex, past bio-geographical population distributions towards the organism's distant past.

The Biological Species Concept defines a species at a specific moment in time. Perhaps the answer is to reconstruct evolutionary histories, where a species is simply the terminal branch of Darwin's carefully drawn Tree of Life in his famous book. Here the bud at the tip of the furthest twig is the finite form of a living thing: fixed in a moment; fleetingly constant; nameable instantly and yet temporarily. Perhaps a true species is a form of life paused only in the blink of our watching eye on its wondrous journey to becoming another form of life; a transitional entity, a wonderful gesture of diversity, defined by a common, recognisable, derived characteristic for our convenience, just once. At any given time in the evolutionary journey of all life forms, we are able to differentiate a species by observing at least one consistent difference between it and related species. This approach to defining a species is called the Phylogenetic Species Concept.

How we determine this difference, however, is a fundamental question, governed only by our level of engagement with the natural world. Is the difference obvious, like the sheen on a hummingbird's neck, or is it microbiological, like a single genetic substitution? Are we to define a species at the molecular level? What if the genetic change does not even influence protein synthesis and is structurally undetectable? How many species would occupy our planet, how would we differentiate them, and how constant would be the number of differing life forms every day and every moment of every day? In his book *The Selfish Gene*, Richard Dawkins explores living things at the genetic scale in terms of units of natural selection, reminding us that species are not stable through evolutionary time, that genetically, species 'are like clouds in the sky... temporary aggregations or federations'.[5]

Perhaps, then, the names of species are merely crude, superficial labels at the mega-scale of the human gaze, mere collective nouns for populations of individuals, clusters of 'survival machines' (in Dawkins's fine new term) for genes. Or should species be described as genetic units, a momentary statistical effect of constantly changing gene frequencies, the lowest common denominators of evolution? This would give them almost immortal status, like the ancient rocks living in geological time.

Ultimately, the definition of a species is very simple. It is whatever we need it to be. It is a night bird on a rolling plain in Nechisar. It is a reflection of our humanity – sometimes a reflection in the deep night or on the deep sea. It is a human construction, our device for naming, built like a giant lighthouse, vigorous, bright and directional, showing the way clearly, safely and loudly. Species are only relevant if they can order a physical comprehension of our living world, if they can assist us in stating and testing biological theories, if they can provide a mechanism for measuring biodiversity. To confer the status of species to a life is to make life itself alive and visible

5 R. Dawkins, *The Selfish Gene*. Oxford University Press, reprinted 2009, p. 33.

to us structurally. In this context – where a myriad of forms live as the menagerie of life, revolving globally as a thriving bubble in universal space – one turns to the birdwatchers: the watchers of wilderness, the listers, counters, readers of names, storytellers. Birdwatchers simplify a relationship with nature into that of observation, comparison and learning. They see, think, question and find deep connection. With them I chart my personal exploration of the wild earth, seeking victory over ignorance, seeking the comfort of belonging among the pristine. I choose the realm of the bird: I look upon open skies of birds, across endless rivers of birds, over great oceans of birds, into high forests and low plains of birds. I look at their great repetitions and great variety, and at their immolations, one thing for another. I look objectively, purposefully and with felicity at the landscapes, so feathered and diverse. And I look to a 'species' as a category of classification and build my definition of nature around it. It is my basic unit, the central concept of birdwatching. And in my definition of species I choose the middle ground: the sure, pragmatic moderate ground that is sound, firm and useful. It is perhaps a compromise, but it is sincere.

When a group of birds reproduces naturally, creating fertile offspring of both genders, I embrace the Biological Species Concept and describe them as a true species. Where two populations look similar but have no contact with each other (or where they establish a clear boundary between their populations despite contact), I embrace the Phylogenetic Species Concept, and see them as true species only if DNA sequencing shows conclusive differences.

Like mating birds on a branch, one must bring together concepts in useful combination, both biological and phylogenetic. And so, as birdwatchers, we list and count birds, sure and accurate in our rules, yet mindful of yesterday and tomorrow, knowing that all species are ultimately connected through descent from a common ancestor. While we watch birds we also know that they are changing. We know they are neither independent of each other nor immutable. From an evolutionary standpoint, the names of birds are arbitrary, yet to those who watch they are emotionally essential.

Bird species are the units that define collections and the view into every landscape. They are the commodities of the trade in memories. They are the bartering products swapped at fireside discussion, the vocabulary of exploration stories and the language of adventure tales. They are a 'value system' and our currency of the wilderness. With them birdwatchers buy understanding and own a place of observation in nature. With them birdwatchers think back to the extinct birds and forward to the new birds of tomorrow. With them we see common birds every day and uncommon birds every other day, and we dream of seeing a rare bird one day: perhaps the bird of Nechisar.

CHAPTER EIGHT
RARA AVIS

OUR NEED TO CATALOGUE the natural world continues. Perhaps we have an instinctive compulsion to identify all that lives. A great gate has been unlocked onto a seemingly infinite place of new sounds and sights, new moving forms of life, big and small. Our momentum is unstoppable. Quixotically, we are confident in the placement of our species within the landscape of a living system. The wilderness, new in its ever-continuing revelation, becomes the very thing that defines us and our way forward as beings who search and name. The more we explore, the more exploration is required up ahead. The more we find, the more exciting it becomes to go on finding. The more we unravel, the more mysteries emerge. The more we look, the more carefully we must look and contemplate – ours is a thinking search. To see new life has become a meticulous search. All those millions of creatures still to be found, still at large, still free and wild are tangibly accessible. Our journey to the new forms of life continues, and the more we discover, the more we are able to compare, organise and determine what is truly rare.

When we consider a 'rarity' in the natural world, we describe life that is interesting and valued because it is uncommon and often tremendously challenging to find and see. The rarity has become of the elite (and of the few). The rarity embodies all that is threatened, and reminds us of a shrinking world. The rarity speaks of evolution and of the fleeting existence of species. The rarity has become a treasured living symbol of the precious, of change. It reminds us of the temporariness of life and of life's different forms. Sprinkled in the wilderness around us, these rarities lie hidden – the special ones, the keepers of the untamed, the last gatekeepers of the pristine.

Is an alluvial diamond sieved from a stream bed rare? To me such rareness is unimportant. Its value is fashioned slickly and unnaturally, translated and defined by money, emerging in carats and cuts, shaped to refract light into bliss for the eyes – the bigger, the better, the rarer. The diamond is financially costly but insignificant, invisible from the angle of wildness, and ultimately worthless to the rareness within the world of biodiversity. It is only a rare, lifeless relic of the land. Rare birds are not like rare diamonds.

Astatine is rare in nature. It is the rarest form of the non-metal element halogen, and it occurs naturally through radioactive decay. There is less than a teaspoonful of astatine on our entire planet and it is treasured because of this scarcity. But for astatine to be seen it must first be extracted. Like the diamond, it must be taken from its place in the earth, leaving a vacancy, a void (however small). It cannot be seen existing freely as can an untouched crystal, a free parrot, an unhindered rock, a floating puff of natural gas. The act of its infinitesimal removal from the wild landscape is our only access to it. We embrace it unnaturally. To see the rareness of astatine is to take from the land in a minuscule plundering; to destroy for the sake of rareness. Seeing rare birds is not like seeing rare astatine.

Rareness is, of course, a human construct. It is our way of describing the special few. But for birdwatchers, celebration is only appropriate when the rare is a living creature of the natural world.

When the rare is part of nature, we begin to understand the relevance of exploration – true exploration – and the importance of discovering wild life. Only then can we honestly find the innocence, the purity of the rare and its resilience. When we look for rare creatures we search with conviction, because ours is a quest for affirmation. When we look upon the rare, diversity is confirmed; and we value the common more (hopefully with sensitivity and care). Ours is the gaze of the polymath. It must be a compassionate, wise look, a glance in awe, a view in hope, a thorough sighting of the last of a kind – the honestly, delicately, significantly rare.

We could search, surely, for rare forms of many different living things: there are rare orchids, worms, monkeys, snakes and slugs. There are rare dragonflies, fish, corals, mushrooms and bacteria. In the vast assemblage of life, with its myriad of branches and sub-branches, rareness has visited all. Rareness is a precursor to extinction, and extinction is part of the evolutionary process. Extinction is as important as life itself – it shapes life, and rareness is our narrator in the story of change.

Birdwatchers choose to search for and look at birds. Birds are our guides to nature, to the pristine. Perhaps we choose them because they have a civil tangibility, measurably accessible to our view of the landscape, and definitive within our understanding of the laws of the landscape. Perhaps birds are sensible to our sensibilities – they are generally easy to see and they are pretty. Birds have become our opportunity to enter the world of the rare: the place of distant little leaves on the Tree of Life. By watching birds we focus on a type of living form, and from within that great variety we begin to see those that are rare. Ours is a contextual awakening within a landscape of feathers and interconnectivity, and from there the profoundness of the rare calls clearly.

With the privilege of looking for rare birds comes the challenge of finding them. Rare birds are rarely seen – the rarest almost never – but while looking for them we must surely and inevitably ask: Which is the rarest bird on earth? Which is the one with that feathered crown? Which deserves the title Monarch of the Named, Winged King (or Queen), Defender of Regal Rareness? Which bird calls to us like the finishing tape to the long-distance runner:

victoriously, defiantly, persistently, enduringly, vitally, desperately, conclusively?

The Black Stilt is a large wading bird. Waders (or shorebirds) are among the most popular birds. They represent the mystery of migration, fanning out annually and seasonally across continents and oceans in an ultimate inhabitation, echoing our joy of travel and discovery. They also represent a challenge in identification. Variance in plumage and shape is often subtle and nuanced. The understanding of these birds is beautifully satisfying, always exciting to the eye and taxing to the mind as we come to unravel breeding and non-breeding colours and patterns. Although the Black Stilt is not a long-distance migrant, and its adult plumage colour remains unchanged all year long, it is nevertheless a special wader, regarded by many as the rarest of them all. And to be so rare and 'of the waders' is to be doubly special, and so it is greatly desired by birdwatchers.

This stilt is found only in New Zealand, where breeding pairs remain inland on the select, braided riverbeds and small streams and tarns of South Canterbury and North Otago. It was called the Kaki by the Maori people of its past, who considered it a *taonga* species – a living treasure. It is elegantly delicate, standing on tight spindles – long red legs so thin that from afar the black body floats like a rugby ball. Its bill is also thin, sharp and needled.

Everything about the bird is hesitant and tenuous; it teeters sharply on the air in a teetering walk and a teetering pause; it teeters on food in a mood of final feeding; and it teeters on the brink of extinction.

Through our modern call for advanced irrigation and drainage schemes, our need for peopled spaces and our consequent demand for hydroelectric developments, we have irreparably disturbed the Black Stilt's habitat and taken away its rivers. Foreign plants have stolen its breeding places. A century ago it walked safely; now it is hunted by alien stoats, weasels, ferrets, cats, rats and even hedgehogs. Today, in its final moments, it meets its congeners infrequently and has begun to mate with other stilts of a different species in obligate confusion. To birdwatchers it appears lonely and lost, selling its genes into oblivion. At one time the Black Stilt was a bird of stability, appropriately abundant, living independently, interconnected in perfect balance, uninterrupted and undisturbed in its graceful pose.

By 1981 the population had declined to twenty-three adult birds, and New Zealand conservation authorities implemented a recovery plan. Birds were studied, eggs were taken, and a population was hand-reared and bred in captivity. Over years of intensive management this population grew, and each year some of the sub-adults were released back to the wild streams. Now the estimated number of mature

Black Stilts wandering free is hoped to be about two hundred and fifty.

This extremely rare species is presently regarded by BirdLife International and the International Union for Conservation of Nature (IUCN) as critically endangered, at risk of imminent extinction. But it is not the rarest bird of them all. Some might say it is not even the rarest wader. The Wirebird of St Helena as well as the Shore Plover and Chatham Islands Oystercatcher, both of the Chatham archipelago, have even smaller populations. Only one or two hundred of each species – maybe fewer – are thought to exist, and species like the Slender-Billed Curlew are still fewer in number.

Most of these extremely rare waders exist on fragile islands where ecosystems embody much of the meaning of rareness, surviving as unique menageries of the vulnerable, precarious habitats of insular geography and insular hope, leftovers of the pure, and dwindling in fecundity. Island waders and other rare island birds have become our reflections as we watch them contemplatively. They remind us of the shrinking wildernesses across our planet. In them we see ourselves, perhaps also isolated and threatened, as final bastions running out of sustainable space and time. In them, perhaps, we see our earth as an island, bobbing in blackness, alone like the stilt, interconnected, troubled and ill, yet still hopeful.

Although some of these island species have always been rare, evolving as tiny populations in remote bliss, most owe their rareness to us. Human history has fashioned extinction like a great quilt, patching and stitching islands together with the common thread of death. Islands once alone and independent, living as unique equilibriums, became bonded in the sick connection of extinction. Satisfying our need to expand civilisation, we colonised archipelago after archipelago, leaving death in the style of a serial killer: patterned, predictable, compulsive and pathetic. Thousands of years of colonisation have witnessed humanity effectively killing off the islands with its suffocating quilt. Isle after isle has become less beautiful and infinitely, tragically changed. Shorelines have lost their sparkle, treelines have lost their colour, and mountain slopes no longer teem with creatures. All is blanketed in loss. Biodiversity is rent.

The history of human encounter with the wondrous birds of islands stinks of ignorance, violence and excess. When humanity arrived two thousand years ago in Madagascar, a huge island birthed from Africa, the first birds to become extinct were the flightless ones: the biggest and most conspicuous, the easiest to see, hunt and eat. The elephant birds, various Aepyornis species, were exterminated. Bird megafauna destruction was absolute. All that remains today are fossilised eggs, large like the land, filled with rock, cracked and shelled and broken. When the big birds were gone, the medium-sized birds were taken next. Other genera and species were taken too. Extinction became a plague; the killing was popular and effortless. Across the Indian Ocean, other examples of this death moved like a powerful wave, unstoppable, uncontrollable. Arriving from the East Indies through Micronesia, Melanesia and Polynesia, humans annihilated almost half of all bird species on these islands. Today this great shroud of death lies incomplete, edged loosely in tattered strands.

Islands are laboratories of extinction and rareness. To see this kind of island rareness, I went to a faraway island in the tropical Mascarene Group. I made my way to Mauritius, the land once trodden by the unfortunate, iconic and famously extinct Dodo. I found Mauritius a sad place, steeped in the memory of annihilation. In many ways it is a typical isle, another example of mindlessness. What makes it sadder is the naïve and shameless celebration of death, with carcinogenic plastic Dodos – cast in factories far across the seas – on sale as bath toys: bright, vulgar symbols of misguided pride. 'Dead as a Dodo' is a money-spinner, a strap-line on cheap T-shirts. Far from mourning such a tragic failure, locals smile and chic visitors laugh. Luxurious inappropriateness abounds at every hotel and on every hotel road.

But there is another Mauritius: remnant Mauritius.

Here extinction is taken seriously and the history of death is a scientific lesson. This Mauritius has heard the warning from its past. Ten million years have seen the island rise volcanically from the ocean to tell the story of wild, evolving populations, rich diversity, adaptation and finally a dogged survival. This Mauritius is vivacious, vital and beautiful. It is a retreat, a place of refuge. It is here that I came to see the triumphant Mauritius Parakeet, another of the rarest birds on earth.

It was, coincidentally, the morning after my marriage, and I stood in an upland dwarf forest on the high mountain slope of the Black River Gorges National Park with my wife Kathleen. It was a special morning and a powerful beginning. The early dawn light reflected from the sea below, funnelling clouds in silver ripples like a vast wedding gift. Tiny white tropic birds fluttered above the valley floor like confetti against the canopy. Stunted, crowded trees reached up from the ground all around us. They were old and very slow-growing, bent into distorted curls and stretched knots, bearded and whimsically draped in soft, green lichen. Trunks creaked in the breeze. Thick, waxy leaves formed unusual umbrella shapes, some even fanned protectively. This was the unforgettable Macchabee Forest.

Kathleen and I walked alone down the exquisitely private hill. Everything was ours to enjoy and everything was shared. The forest hugged us in camaraderie, the trees close and intimate. We engaged with the landscape in complete matrimony.

Then a screech ripped the sky above the trees. A long-tailed parakeet burst overhead, hurtling in a wide green tumbling circle as if a piece of the forest had become detached, like a branch in the wind, torn and uncomfortably exposed. Then it was gone, sucked from sight.

I had never seen such a green. It was the precious green of the emerald, only rarer, less stereotyped and even more valuable, oddly translucent and three-dimensional, refracting light like a window opening onto a wild view. The green revealed a pigmented structure designed by the forest. For me it was also highly symbolic. Green is the colour of Greenpeace and green politics, of Animal Planet and BBC Earth, of eco-labels and green energy. It is the colour of conscience and human concern for the environment.

In 2010, scientists estimated that there were about three hundred of these parakeets left in the wild, all here in this island, the last sanctuary of this species. The Mauritius Parakeet was for a time the world's most endangered bird: in 1986 fewer than twelve such birds lived free, only three of which were female. But captive breeding and reintroduction programmes were implemented with rigour and conviction over many years. What flew above us that morning was not only rareness, but also a living testament to conservation success.

My wife and I walked further down the hill, deeper into the forest. The bird called again, this time from a perch in a clearing. It was at home on the tree, comfortable as a child on a jungle gym. It lifted its leg and stretched, unfolding one wing downwards. Now we could see the whole bird in its completeness. From the top of its head to the tip of its long tail, it was all a brilliant green. Then, very subtly, a shadow borrowed blueness from the sky, fringing the feathers so that all was infused with blue. This was my first green-blue bird. Its blue shimmer waved like the coral fringe of the island, blending the blue of the sea with the green of the land – island colours for my first real island bird. Through my mind flitted thoughts of natural history, naturalism, the dispersal of species, isolation, environmental pressure, speciation and the radiation of life – and I smiled like Darwin. Slowly, surely and knowingly, the parakeet revealed a ring of black feathers around its neck, hinting at a pink edge like a fresh, friendly smile. The bird leaned forward, pulled by its big, red beak – the strong, important beak of an important parrot. It was the red of danger, the red of the IUCN Red List on which this parrot has just been downgraded to 'endangered' from 'critically endangered' – less rare for just a moment.

For this rare island bird, firm conservation

strategies were now in place. The Mauritius Parakeet remained a very rare bird, but no longer the rarest bird on earth. Yet for me, a sad absurdness and ambiguity had accompanied their rescue. Their once-wild home was now a zoo of documentation. And I began to see the bird differently.

A tag hung from a ring on the bird's leg, bearing a name or number. Below it the tree was strategically pruned and bandaged tightly in shiny black plastic. This tree (like the island) was overrun with rats, and the slippery plastic, like a moat around a castle, protected the birds from invasion. Above the bird was a factory-made nest box, its right angles at odds with the forest, the perfect circle of its entrance hole so perfectly out of place. Orderly landscaped paths provided viewing platforms and signposted trails. This well-trodden site survived on ecotourism and human curiosity. Conservation and concern hung heavy in the air, but the fake had been substituted for the feral. Survival of the species had been bought at a price, and the bird flew invisibly caged.

On my walk down the gorge to the ocean I encountered other rare birds in conservation. Some had always been rare because of their limited range and habitat; others had been made rare by human arrival; all were now rarer from human pressure. The Pink Pigeon population had dropped to ten by 1991, and was now three hundred and classed 'endangered' on the IUCN Red List. The Mauritius Kestrel hit a low of just four birds in 1974 and was now eight hundred to a thousand birds and 'vulnerable'. The three hundred Mauritius Fodys were 'endangered', and both the Mauritius Black Bulbul and the Mauritius Cuckooshrike were 'vulnerable'.

As numerically rare as all these birds were, their intimate proximity to us on that Mauritian morning made them seem populous and accessible amid this crowded landscape of sugarcane, roads, peopled plots, loud hotels and frenetic consumer streets.

Surely a greater rareness than this is to be rare in a pristine wilderness, to be wildly rare and free.

*

The Galapagos Islands nestle like ships from an eternal storm, a place of extreme isolation and a harbour for the very rare. Over aeons they have offered a fathomable shelter and an opportunity for the colonising few to dock, develop and divide, and thence to radiate and speciate as if gently pushed by the tide.

We cruised across the Bolivar Channel on a sea of fertility: as humpbacks sounded, a manta slid beneath us, fishes flapped into the sky and boobies dived into the water. The channel was framed on either side by islands, protecting it from the Pacific.

To port lay Fernandina, a simmering new lava shield; to starboard towered the older Isabela. These great volcanic rocks of life leaned up from the ocean into the sky, steaming, hissing and creaking in their growing pains. Born of heat through cracks in the earth's crust, they oozed into mountains of diversity while their blackness slowly morphed into black sand for the green mangroves.

We had come to see the critically endangered Mangrove Finch, a species with possibly fewer than eighty birds left on earth. They are only found on Isabela now, gone forever from Fernandina but for a single sighting in 2009 by my bird-guide friend Andreas. On Isabela they remain in a few small, isolated populations restricted to particular patches of mangrove swamp that are separated by deserts of hardened lava. These oases of trees that sustain the Mangrove Finch are subtly different from the other swamps along the seashore. Detached from the suck of the ocean tide, their leaf litter is never washed out, leaving a forest floor rich in dead wood that fashions a bed of leaves for breeding and feeding. Only in this unique world of tall mangroves and dry leaf layers can the Mangrove Finch exist. Amid a desert of black rock, these leaves lie like a pond of fresh water, defining a miniature, self-contained world. As in any desert haven, they exist in powerful juxtaposition: soft and hard; food and famine; wet and dry; shade and light; cool and hot; finch life and finch death.

Scientists say there may be only two swamp forests of these finches left, and that these two remaining populations are in dangerous decline. These two small groups, separated already for about a hundred years, have begun to differentiate into new species. Perhaps they are already unrecognisable to one another: calling out in foreign songs from foreign forests in estranged calls of eternal dissociation. Perhaps they have now become a unproductively unviable new species.

These separate populations also struggle with other foreignness – the arrival of alien cats, rats, ants, wasps, birds, parasites and human beings. An alien poison has permeated their world; it is a subtle poison and time is its friend. It infests, sucks life, destroys habitat and hope, eating away at the finch and its future. A season of destruction is unfolding on Isabela. And in this season we sailed towards the shoreline to seek out the special finch in its rareness.

Our access permit specified where we were allowed to go ashore. Its rules were clear and unambiguous, part of an environmental antidote to resuscitate the pristine and rescue threatened island species, offering them time to heal and science time to find long-term solutions to the destructive effects of invasive alien species. We paid great respect to these rules.

Our ship waddled seventy metres from the edge of the island, where a line of little waves defined a beach of black sand. This was Playa Tortuga Negra and its hard black border formed an unbreachable barrier – we were not permitted to leave the boat. Black rocks disappeared into black water in a gentle heave of the sea; black grains of lava made a shore that became black ripples of ocean; blackness made reflections of black light on the high slopes of the nearby hills; black pebbles became black cliffs; and looming walls of lava stretched skyward under the sun like giant charred limbs. Exploding from the black leapt bright bunches of mangroves, glowing like green sweat on the rocks. We were close enough to make out the texture of the leaves and close enough to scan for birds. Gazing deeply through binoculars and spotting scopes, we probed ever deeper, crowding the rocking deck of the boat with tripods and lenses and dreams of the finch.

My companions were Mel Tripp and Clide Carter, and this finch would be a lifer for us all. Clide had seen nearly eight thousand bird species across the world, and as he searched the trees he pulled with his eyes – lifers are few and far between when you have enjoyed so many already. Mel, a well-known South African birdwatcher, hovered like a dragonfly as if winged by the breeze, his forehead glistening with anticipation. I held my binoculars to my face like a mask: a warrior garbed for victory. Hours passed, and the incessant sway of the sea tapped on the hull like a hollow clock. All was stationary on land apart from a Galapagos Mockingbird, a species we had encountered many times on the other islands over the past week. Gradually the black landscape became blacker, and the Mangrove Finch eluded us. This threatened species with its extremely small population and no captive-breeding programme is indeed very rare, but its numbers suggest that it is not yet the rarest of the rare.

There are other very rare birds with still smaller world numbers that are not yet conserved at all. Surely these birds are even rarer than those linked to us through conservation programmes. Surely among these other endangered species, where we watch from afar, remotely, where there are no rules to control access, where we are less facilitated and assisted, where human visits are less regular, more difficult and more dangerous, surely here must live the very rarest of the rare: the pure and unsullied rare.

*

The Sidamo Lark is thought to live only on the Liben Plain of south-eastern Ethiopia, although the land here slides towards Somalia in unexplored remoteness. This is a harsh land, unsettling and unsettled, far from everywhere and barely known to humanity. The lark lives here amid war and famine, hunched low, close to the ground, cryptic and resilient. It is so much a part of the ground that some even call it the Liben Lark. To know this lark is to know the ground of this plain and its delicate seasons, delicate rains and the flimsiness of life. The grass is low, even the soil is low; all appears short and squashed under the sun. Life here is subtle, and observing it requires a careful, undistracted focus.

It took us many days to get to the Liben Plain, many long brown days of driving from Addis Ababa before we finally stood on the plain. It was framed in the distance by dense brown acacia woodland, marking the edge of the home of the lark: forty square kilometres in all. This is its world, it is found nowhere else, we think. There are none in captivity, no other populations. This is the rarest lark in the world, isolated and (predictably) also brown.

We had learnt of its rareness because less than fifty birds are thought to remain. It is seldom airborne because it is uncomfortable in the sky. Its long neck and long legs give it a dangling awkwardness. Neither in normal flight nor in display flight is it aerodynamic, a trait that has limited its ability to disperse. Unable to roam and find new homes, it is now trapped, confined to a single tiny tract of land. It has become a relic, a memory of a past habitat, a memory of change.

The pastoral community in the area has increased its cultivation and grazing over past decades, and there has been military activity and war. I looked up at the sun, just enough to feel it on my face, and there was just one tree with one shadow. I looked out at the small huts and small people at the edges of the plain. Then I looked inward and understood the shrinking world of the Sidamo Lark. I saw that this was a bird fast running out of time, and wondered how many more suns it would see. I sensed extinction – this could be the first bird to become extinct on mainland Africa in my time.

I desperately wanted to see this lark, to tell people I had seen it, to share the story of its life and its death. I hoped to share a message of the transitory nature of rareness and the importance of conserving the rare. We spread out and looked on the ground, waiting for it to move revealingly.

Then a bird ran, suddenly high among all that was low. It stopped upright, paused and stretched. It was urgent. It was without a shadow. It had an almost triangular head atop a thin neck, dark-crowned and dark-eyed, peering past us darkly. It had known other big creatures on the plain, I thought. It ran forward and behind it I saw a nest: twisted into the soil with circles of grass, flush with the surface, a hollow cupped into the earth with three little eggs, flecked and brown and vulnerable.

I will never forget this brown lark and its nest. I honour it here, but it was not the rarest of the rare.

It was completely free and still untamed. It was completely feral and able to breed wildly. It was still part of a natural system, however threatened. It could still be reached reliably – although with difficulty, danger and discomfort – and it could still be watched in a macabre alliance of hope and celebration. Science had finally come to know it and might still offer it a possible future. Some even think that another population lives sheltering on another plain, perhaps a safer one. It is not the rarest bird on earth, not yet. There are others that are rarer, with less opportunity, less time, less wilderness.

Some birds no longer exist in the wild. They probably do not make nests beyond captivity. They are not known to fly freely and their caged populations are only a vestigial memory of a wild species, like a single feather floating detached, like an empty eggshell, a landscape without life. These birds are so scarce that they are probably beyond birdwatching: to birdwatchers they fall into the world of the unseeable. For birdwatchers the future of such birds can only lie in the natural world. If there is to be a temporary life of captivity for a species followed by reintroduction into their natural habitat – the act of reinventing the rare – it will be flavoured by history, and a past life will have to be reshaped into a distant opportunity for possible, future rareness. Only then might these birds begin to reoccupy their place on the list of the very rare again, the wildly rare.

Spix's Macaw is such a bird. In 1817 Dr Johann Baptist Ritter von Spix was exploring a remote woodland along the banks of a river in the north-east of Bahia, Brazil. It was an unexplored place, thorny and sharp, but birds flew there, some as blue as the Atlantic over which he had sailed, their blueness made bluer by the dust and the leaflessness. This peculiar woodland was called Caatinga by the local people, and it was unique because it had made a blue parrot.

A flock flew past Spix, their long tails trailing, the sky alive with feathers. He shot and collected one of these birds as a way of learning. It was an honourable engagement then in order to examine, study, file, understand and remember. And one day, about fifteen years later, the bird was named after him.

Even then this macaw was a rare species. Even before greed displaced enquiry and possession replaced collection, these exquisite birds were inherently rare.

Spix's Macaw is every shade of blue. Its pale blue head and belly are the blues of Picasso; its deep blue wings and tail are the blues of Van Gogh. These are wise blues, sad blues, thoughtful blues and crazy blues, all rich in considered imagery as if made from the brush lines of a master, and yet each blue feather is a painterly stroke of genius; each blue changes the mood of the mind like the hues of a song, translucent and shifting like a backlit ocean wave. Each blue captures greed and desire like a sapphire, ultimately seducing us tragically. If ever blues have conjured melancholy, none have done so more than those of Spix's Macaw.

This magnificent wild species was hunted and pillaged in a frenzy of avarice. Collectors of cage birds so coveted it that just a hundred and eighty years after its discovery it was extinct in the wild, although habitat destruction and the aggressive alien African bee played their part. Today this macaw knows only the shadows of wire mesh, flying in stunted space, feeding from seed trays and fruit pots. Today it mates ashamedly for money. Our greed for its beauty has ultimately stolen this bird from the wild.

The last three wild birds (two adults and a chick) were captured for the pet trade in December 1987. In July 1990 a single wild male was discovered bizarrely pairing with a female Blue-Winged Macaw. Then in 1995, with renewed hope and excitement, ornithologists released a female Spix's Macaw from a captive population into the study site, where it began to pair with the male. Luck and chance danced happily with science in an important moment for the story of rareness. But weeks later the female disappeared. Some spoke of a blueness severed sharply from the sky by a power line, a fatal flight, a pathetic shredding of the last of a kind, and after 2000 the lonely male was never seen again. Now the Caatinga cries appropriately. Today there is a coordinated captive breeding programme under-way, managed by the Brazilian government, and the unofficial number of birds in cages is thought to be about a hundred and twenty. Yet the occasional rumoured sighting of a lone bird filters in from remote forests, and dreams hover hopefully again for the wild rareness of Spix's Macaw. One day this bird may become the rarest bird on earth, but today it waits tentatively for its freedom – along with a few others, including the Hawaiian Crow, whose remaining fifty-three birds exist in captivity. Today Spix's Macaw is not the rarest bird on earth.

*

There are birds that were seen by birdwatchers many years ago and known to be rare, and then suddenly were gone, their extinction instantaneous.

In the moments before the death of the last of a species there is an awful lingering (for us), a sick lull, immersed in powerlessness, like the strong, silent suck of the sea before the rise of a wave, the stillness between the screams of prey in a deep forest – that quiet void before death. In those moments of anticipation (which sometimes last years) there is a kind of pre-extinction, the knowledge that what lives before you will never be again, without descent or descendants, the end of an intricate link in the web of life. And we feel tremendous awkwardness, perhaps shame, as it moves in utter rareness for just a few moments more. And then, like a shooting star, it is gone. Our gaze drifts back to the reassuring celestial twinkling of all the life that remains – a little dimmer ever after.

One by one these birds have claimed the title of the rarest bird on earth. One by one their rareness fuelled the urgency of conservation, reminding us of the preciousness of life and our apparent helplessness. And one by one they disappeared forever. Perhaps the conservation efforts were naïve, the threat of extinction underestimated. Now these birds exist only in old photographs and drawings, field notes and stories. Yet sometimes birds may reappear after we have proclaimed them extinct.

Wilderness can appear stubborn, indignant. We like to imbue it with personality; regarding it alternately as our mother or our foe. But in truth, we are simply a small part of this great living system. At these times we are reminded of our place as observers. Nature is the Great Prestidigitator, the master of tricks; we are mere components of a whole that we cannot control – a timeless and ever-changing, revealing, renewing, adapting, evolving oscillation. Much in nature is still wildly foreign to us. Much of the pristine still exists in isolation from us, withheld like sight from the blind. The pristine environment may be shrinking geographically, but it is still an intensely private place. And so, from time to time, extinct birds step out of that unknown, like powerful recollections of the past. At these times we are humbled, and reminded of why it is so important to keep watching the rare.

On 1 November 2006, a team of conservationists made their way along a remote lake-edge in northern Madagascar. It was a small, high lake, a shallow bowl of water in the crater of an old volcano. Its water was still, holding its secrets quietly, its colours modest and muddy like the shades of dust and mist. All was earthy, subtle and blurred. It was called Matsaborimena by the rural people, but they did not go there – the water was cold, it held no fish and its sides were not fertile for farming. It was unexplored.

Then the lake rippled. A duck popped up in a bubble of bobbing feathers. Like a ball it bounced on the rhythm of the lake, and wobbled shallowly as if dribbled by an imaginary foot. It was a diving duck, brown-backed and white-eyed, and off its feathers rolled little balls of water glistening like jewels.

This bejewelled duck was the famously extinct Madagascar Pochard, whose last single male had last been sighted many years before. And although old notes said the species was usually solitary, the duck was not alone. Eight more adults and four juveniles appeared before the startled eyes of these birdwatchers as the Madagascar Pochard suddenly came back to life.

At this site of its rediscovery we now see it swimming presciently, breeding safely and successfully. Its numbers are now presumed to be over fifty and slowly increasing. Its proud journey through great rareness has taught us much. But it is no longer the rarest bird on earth. Other species of bird have also been rediscovered recently. The Kinglet Cotinga, last seen in the nineteenth century, was rediscovered in 1996; the Golden-Crowned Manakin, not seen since its discovery in 1957, reappeared in 2002; the New Zealand Storm Petrel, known only from sub-fossil material and three nineteenth-century specimens, was seen in 2003; the Long-Legged Thicketbird, not seen since 1894, was rediscovered in 2003.

Perhaps other birds that are presumed extinct exist somewhere still. To be possibly extinct is to move towards greater rareness, and perhaps even beyond rareness. It is to become part of the possibly very rare and the probably non-existent. The Po'ouli of the Hawaiian island of Maui is such a bird. That it might still exist gives an urgent relevance and a distant desperate hope of rareness – a last hope.

In 1973 students from the University of Hawaii climbed the steep slope of a volcanic mountain called Haleakalā, and in a great shadow on the wet, windward watershed they discovered this bird, hidden like a secret amid the dark green of a dense, tangled rainforest – a refuge of thick, clinging mountain branches and lush mountain leaves. The shadow of the crater wall was home to special soils and new creatures. Haleakala, meaning 'house of the sun', was remote and seldom visited. Perhaps the ancient light from the volcano had made the shadow protectively, casting a wall to keep people out. It was dark like the blackouts of war, like segregation and censorship. The shadow rolled in over moss overhangs, over olapa and ohi'a lehua trees, over ferns coiled like giant springs waiting to be sprung. Within this shadow lived the Po'ouli, independent and inaccessible, hopping secretively as it fed on tree snails, spiders and insects.

The Po'ouli belongs to a famous, endemic group of Hawaiian birds called honeycreepers; its other name is the Black-Faced Honeycreeper, and it is oddly finch-like with white cheeks, short wings and a stub tail. At the time of its discovery there were thought to be only two hundred of them on that slope. It was their only habitat, a world defined by a single, shrinking shadow. By 1995 only five (or maybe seven) were known, and by 1997 only three – two males and a female. This little black-faced bird was sliding downhill towards oblivion. Years passed and the three birds lived independently of each other, territorially, each flitting in its own part of the forest, shaded separately, yet united in a single tragedy. The mountain became a sad place of division, enclosed now in a steel fence of scientific optimism, yet still subdivided by the invisible fences of instinct. In 2002, in an attempt to encourage breeding, the female was captured and released into the home range of a male. Hours later the female returned to her own territory, uninterested.

On 9 September 2004 a male was captured and taken to the Maui Bird Conservation Center in an attempt to start a captive-breeding programme. But a mate could not be found. The little flying shadows had finally disappeared, succumbing to isolation and death.

The lone bird died in a plastic container on 26 November. The Po'ouli has never been seen again. It is now listed as 'critically endangered' by BirdLife International, a cautionary gesture in case it might still exist. This status is conservative, uncomfortable and possibly political. Most ornithologists consider it extinct; therefore it cannot be considered the rarest bird on earth. It hovers too uneasily, like a mythical apparition, like a sighting of Elvis at a party. It probably lives on only as a story now: a parable for conservationists, a failed experiment by scientists and a sad narrative for birdwatchers.

At this edge of rareness, teetering on uncertainty,

we must also look further back into history to the birds presumed extinct for an even longer time; ones we still talk and write about after many, many years, those that still inhabit our faraway hope of being the rarest of all – those that refuse to leave our dreams, those that might just have been sighted again recently in muffled interactions between us and wilderness, those that murmur to us seductively – and we rock uneasily on a precipice of desire where credibility dances with fantasy.

These birds pervade our thoughts like failure. Their images scatter like dead tips of a fractured tree – the Tree of Life. They are among the fringes of the furthest branches of biodiversity, waiting like buds urging to burst, waiting to be found and seen again. They are birds like the Ivory-Billed Woodpecker, the Pink-Headed Duck, the Paradise Parrot and the haunting Eskimo Curlew.

The Eskimo Curlew is said to have guided Christopher Columbus to the New World five centuries ago. It was first described to science in 1772 from a dead specimen by a naturalist who had sailed with Captain Cook, Johann Reinhold Forster. The specimen had been discovered on Hudson Bay and given to him. At that time, after nesting in the Arctic tundra in the northernmost reaches of North America each year, millions of Eskimo Curlews would migrate to the pampas grasslands of South America. Vast mists of these small American curlews with striped heads, mottled brown bodies and downward-curved beaks would fly like seeds tossed into the sky, sown by instinct, riding routes to the south, high and undulating like clouds in the wind. The Eskimo Curlew was an elegant flyer, visible and extravagant, easy for people to see and shoot. Every year between 1850 and 1890, over two million of these birds are thought to have been shot, and soon the spring sky was emptier and less interesting above America. By 1939, the Eskimo Curlew was no more.

On the Texan shoreline of the Gulf of Mexico lies the Galveston Island State Park, a 'barrier island habitat' that is visited by great hurricanes and also by shorebirds. It is a mosaic of bayous, coves, lakes, marshy sheaths, dunes and plains of sand carpeted in grass, and here vast numbers of migrating birds sweep in like storms from the sea to rest during their transcontinental journeys.

One day in 1962 a bird was photographed in this birdwatching refuge as it stood prodding and feeding on the grass like the Lone Star of Texas. It was an Eskimo Curlew. The species had come alive again.

The following year a hunter stood at sunset on the thin coast of Barbados, with a view almost to the horizon, watching carefully as the birds flew towards him in a long row. Flying at the head of the flock was a single bird, divided and different. He squeezed the trigger and it dropped. Instead of eating it, however, he placed it in a deepfreeze, and later gave it to a birdwatcher named James Bond. It was an Eskimo Curlew.

Over the years there have been a few other sightings: one in Guatemala in 1977 and twenty-three in Texas in 1981. Other sightings have been less certain: a possible sighting in Saskatchewan in 1982; another possible adult and juvenile in Alaska in 1983; six possibly in the Northwest Territories in 1985; another in Nova Scotia in 2006. Further rumours have arisen, but now all is quiet again. Yet possible rareness remains out there on the migration routes, and the Eskimo Curlew is very close to being called the rarest bird on earth.

But there are still rarer birds. A bird seen only once by science is surely an extremely rare bird – maybe even the rarest of them all. The White-Chested Tinkerbird is one such bird. It is known from just a single specimen collected in north-western Zambia in 1964. This small, stout-bodied bird with its heavily shaped bill is just two-thirds the size of the everyday sparrow of our towns. In paintings (it has never been photographed) the white stripe on its cheeks forms a teasing smile. It is black above and white below, and the golden yellow of its flanks and the edges of its flight feathers lend a certain glitz, the glitz of the exclusive. But perhaps it is just fool's gold.

I once went looking for this bird at the invitation of Ian Sinclair. Along with the pilot and Dawie and Margo Chamberlain we were five adults, all crushed together in a flimsy airplane almost as tiny as the bird we were after. Paint peeled from the wings and the thin steel skin around us sucked in cold air through multiple cracks, while the pilot farted incessantly and chewed his thumbnail until it bled.

Feeling foreign, aloof and small, we buzzed in detachment above the tightly closed jungle canopy where leaf pressed against leaf in an impermeable, shimmering shield that excluded the sun and us. Above it we bounced along like a stone kicked by a child, skipping from the known to the unknown, random, unnoticed, irrelevant.

Inside the forest, space was tight too. This was Africa's densest forest, dominated by tall, dry evergreen trees, rooted in an impenetrable scrub that tangled and strangled. It was a dry forest that neither spoke nor acknowledged us. It moved anonymously, unquenched and soundless but alive with bees – tiny black dots that buzzed, tickled annoyingly, filling our mouths and blurring our vision.

After many hot, sticky days in that uncomfortable forest we never did find the White-Chested Tinkerbird. Yet we found other things, other answers in the pristine, as birdwatchers always do. Our search for the tinkerbird was also a gesture of respect for the pristine – respect for equilibrium, for purity, for the untouched. Searching enquiringly, steeped in a willingness to learn, we felt a connection with biodiversity and an appreciation of species. Our excitement at the hope of finding the bird became its own reward, and when we did not find it, our attempt itself became a confirmation of wild ownership. Perhaps the mysteries of the bird were to remain unshared in a bold statement that defines true wilderness. The documentation of not finding a bird provides valuable scientific data in itself; and our expedition became a fond memory of rareness, with the memory of the hunt as our trophy.

Some call this bird an aberrant example of a common species, a single bird that merely hatched into life with bizarre plumage – a mutant, a colour morph – thus disqualifying it from the list of the rare. Others revel in it as a bird with new secrets yet to be revealed one day: an importantly rare species. Some might say that this bird does not exist anymore; it might be dead and distinctly extinct. At the very least it lives today as a museum skin, and we know it was once seen flying freely in the wild in 1964. So let it remain on the list of the rarest birds: those species that have been seen only once in birdwatching.

Sometimes there are birds that appear briefly as a mirage; they shimmer on heat in a complex hovering; they confuse and excite and intrigue. They seem to exist as a temporary blur, gluing the vast sky to the vast land in a bizarre covenant of hope. They make our thoughts sweat and our minds float expectantly. They are as tantalising and deeply rejuvenating as an oasis.

One such bird is the Bulo Burti Boubou. In August 1988 it hopped out from behind a dry acacia bush in the grounds of a hospital near Buuloburde, a small town in eastern Somalia. It was black-backed as befitted a boubou (a type of African bush-shrike) with a white eyebrow stripe like many a boubou, but its yellow throat and breast were like none other in those parts. As it hopped territorially in the scrubby thicket around the hospital, a man began to notice it regularly and note what he saw. He wondered about its rareness and imagined it as a new species to ornithology and to birdwatching.

In January 1989, after much discussion, the bird was captured in a mist net. Then the team had a unique idea, as unique as the bird, and perhaps more important than the discovery of the bird. They decided not to kill the boubou as a type specimen for laboratory analysis and systematic filing in a museum drawer. Instead the living bird would be sent to Europe in a cage so that blood samples could be taken and feathers carefully removed, after which it would be returned and released back into its natural habitat near where it had been captured.

Fourteen months later the bird was freed from captivity and flew back like a celebrity into birdwatching fame. This was the first time ever that a new bird species had been described to science as a living sample, as a 'living type', the sole, living, scientific representative of a species. Its Latin name *liberatus* spoke partly of its uniqueness, meaning 'the liberated one'. Perhaps it was a lesson on freedom to Somalia, to Africa and to all who watch nature through birds. The Bulo Burti Boubou became the rarest bird on earth.

Then, in the shimmer of a desert vista in the heat, it was gone, never to be seen again. In 2008, a review of its DNA sequence identified it as a mere colour variant of the Somali Boubou, and it flitted from the world of utter rareness – without stopping at extinction – into a netherworld of never having existed at all. In an instant it became forever irrelevant, a mere shadow of another species. DNA analysis had undone its rareness.

Occasionally, however, DNA analysis has actually conferred rareness. Parrots have spread across the Australian landscape like leaping rainbows. Across this great continental width, two particular populations of parrots have parted slowly, as if with a lazy yawn. One population hugs the far east, the other the far west. This particular species, the Ground Parrot, has a world population of over a hundred thousand. Endemic to Australia, it is one of the world's four ground-dwelling parrot species. This is a bird of reeds, low bushes and grass; it does not like trees. It is green as grass, barred busily in black with a tail as long as a reed. Scientists have studied its two separate populations and wondered evolutionarily. DNA analysis has revealed that the difference is significant: physical distance has brought physical change, but the two species might have come from one. The DNA message appears to have decoded a distinctness, suggesting that the birds of the west should be renamed the Western Ground Parrot and the birds of the east the Eastern Ground Parrot. But as the western population has only about a hundred individuals in danger of imminent extinction, DNA analysis has produced instant rareness.

To find the rarest bird of all, however, we must return to the most rarely seen birds – those few that have been seen only once. We can ponder those that are known from a single specimen, like the Lanai Hookbill, collected in 1914 in Hawaii and then extirpated (although there were technically two further sightings in 1916 and 1918). We can fantasise about the Liverpool Pigeon of French Polynesia collected between 1783 and 1823, known from one specimen now in the Merseyside County Museum in England, and one other specimen that has been lost. We can contemplate Vaurie's Nightjar known from a single record of a female taken in 1929 in Xinjiang, western China. But these birds exist only as ephemeral species, confusing the outer limits of past rareness.

To see the ultimately and significantly rare, we must look to a more recent date of discovery, where hope of a sighting is stronger and opportunity still calls in vital birdsong.

We must think of the Red Sea Cliff-Swallow, known only from the type specimen found dead in 1984 below the Sanganeb lighthouse in the Sudan. Swallows are beautifully aerial and cosmopolitan, occurring on every continent except Antarctica. Many are continental or intercontinental travellers, transient mysteries as they drift like clouds across the sky to uncertain destinations. But when the journey of that single swallow was interrupted at the lighthouse, it fell and left us a riddle. The bird's specific name, *perdita*, means 'lost'. Nothing is known of this species with its shiny black back and throat, its dark grey rump and its pale breast and belly. We know neither where it came from nor where it was going. Some speculate that it lives in the soft hills of the Sudan beside the Red Sea; others say in the remote hills of Eritrea; still others suggest the coastal hills of western Saudi Arabia, where two unidentified but similar swallows were once seen flying towards Jeddah. There is also talk of a strange swallow above Ethiopia, with sightings near Lake Langano in November 1988; at

Awash National Park between 1988 and 1994; in the western highlands of Gibe Gorge between 1993 and 1999; and at Jimma in March 1994. The Red Sea Cliff-Swallow may live in Ethiopia, it may turn and disappear against bright clouds and then reappear again against dark cliffs, sowing confusion as it roams in secret swallowness. It may possibly be the rarest bird on earth.

But Ethiopia holds another bird in even greater rareness: a bird about which there are no stories, no rumours, no myths, and whose origin and whereabouts are unknown; a bird never seen alive, nor seen complete even in death; the only bird on earth described to science by no more than a single wing. This bird is the Nechisar Nightjar.

CHAPTER NINE
FEATHER CROWN

WE SAT IN THE EARLY MORNING light under a red flame tree in Arba Minch, dappled in happiness, the kind that hops around inside the gut, appearing and disappearing in thoughts and murmurs. Fleeting discussions darted like light through a tree, in shades and flashes, some bright, some dark, all gently red in urgency and importance. The excitement of the night before enveloped us like a blanket. We had come to know pure rareness at last. Ian sipped coffee tinged with whisky. Dennis smiled up at the rich orange-red flowers above that thrust up towards the sun like trophies. Gerry stirred a pulpy mango drink coloured like parts of the flowers, and I puffed happily on my cigar. As we fell silent for a while, a tame little duiker – a tiny antelope – fed peacefully on a piece of fruit under our table, its lower jaw rocking sideways as it chewed contentedly like a child with a toffee.

We had not slept much but we had slept well. The Nechisar Nightjar now lived for us as the King of the Rare (the bird of the previous night had been a male). But now, to prove our find to the world, we had unanimously decided in the kind of nodding unison that comes from a precious shared bond and a deep understanding of each other as a team – perhaps even with a tinge of humour – to catch and photograph it as evidence for those who might not believe our story. A find this big was too significant to science and to other birdwatchers to keep to oneself in private notes and thoughts, too momentous to retain only as a tick on a list, too alive not to set free. For my own sanity I needed to release it.

Gerry threw a mango skin into the sun and Wacko – our name for the duiker – wandered after it.

'We need to make a net,' someone finally said.

'On the end of a bloody long pole,' added Ian. He understood the practicalities of making useful things in this part of Africa, and spoke as if he had thought about making nets many times before.

Gerry stood up; he preferred to walk up and down and talk to himself while thinking, perhaps kicking at things in the dust, swearing and looking up at the sky. His bald head became bright in the light as he walked off, and an idea came to him immediately. Gobeze knew people in the town – he had waved to a man earlier and sat laughing with others next to an old shed. He could spread the word and begin a hunt for net-making materials. Gerry had a net design in his head. We called, and Gobeze came running from the other side of the compound where he had been standing quietly on a mound looking out at the distant mountains. He was smiling, and I think he was anxious to share in the excitement of the nightjar sighting. I think he understood us after that night and wanted to be with us under the red tree.

Gerry, who could speak Amharic quite well, discussed with Gobeze the things we would need, filling in the gaps with his hands and arms. He whipped a long imaginary stick about, whacking it towards the ground so convincingly that even the dust jumped and a colourful butterfly lifted. Gobeze grinned, shook Gerry's hand and hugged him before setting off. Then Gerry and I decided to walk into town and see what we could find in preparation for the afternoon's expedition back onto the Nechisar Plains. I liked walking into towns with Gerry; he had a way of talking me through a town like others talked through a problem. He walked analytically, his steps prodding, speaking to people, asking questions and reading the town the way one reads a book.

The town of Arba Minch appeared to have slid lazily downhill. It sat like an old person, a little tired and askew but contented. Its structures, built with wooden frames and mud, had endured many years of use and neglect, and the streets were edged in badly painted broken bricks. Dust covered everything in a thin red-brown film, crinkled and translucent like tissue paper. Where we entered through the outskirts, the once-high rainforest was now low and decapitated: the rich, fertile soil had turned to loose dust and charcoal stains marked where trees had stood. In town many walls and facades were planked and poled with the torn limbs of trees, as if the forest had been used while still alive; one building had green leaves growing from the wood as if the forest was trying to reincarnate itself.

As I walked from the pristine onto the spoiled, tamed earth, I felt powerfully motivated to bring the story of the nightjar back to my world: the often sad, poisoned world of people. It was a story of resilience and hope – of nature's survival, of the rare. I was uncomfortable walking into town; I felt more foreign than I had felt anywhere before, even with Gerry talking beside me. Africa can make one feel like this, perhaps because Africa so vividly conveys the contrast between wild and tame, between people and wilderness. In Africa these two worlds still live so close together, so intimately, their separation so fresh, so recent. The juxtaposition is raw and tremendously sensitive. Or maybe Africa has always been two worlds. There is a lingering and a hesitation at the edges of African towns, like a translucent shroud of dust. Perhaps there is still a chance for instinctive Africa to reunite its parts and find its memories and its equilibrium once more. Birdwatching has made me a strangely proud ambassador of all such ancient and remote towns, not just those in Africa. I felt like a spanning bridge and I vowed to link in honourableness. I wanted to educate.

Arba Minch was a busy town. Corrugated metal floated on mutant sticks, making flimsy shade. Foods and wares for sale were stacked and packed, inhabiting the outside and the in-between, basket piled upon basket, cloths draped like washing. Children clambered on top of each other and tumbled around in the dust. The market talked in many tongues, and business took place amid the noise and confusion.

Massed at the top of a leafless tree were thin sticks bearing Marabou Storks, all clacking their beaks, wobbling pendulous red gullets and shitting out endless white splutter. Beneath the tree like a human stork stood a man with only one leg. Gerry enquired of the old man what had happened to his leg, and he explained that he had lost it as a boy when the rainforest burned.

On a tabletop stood a box of mosquito nets looking as out-of-place as I was. The box was plastered in shiny plastic stickers bearing foreign aid messages. It had clearly been opened many seasons ago, yet still brimmed with nets and misunderstanding. Gerry paid for a net and then purchased a broomstick. On our way back from the town we came across some wire, completing the requirements for Gerry's nightjar net.

Back at camp we found Ian and Gobeze loading equipment into the 4x4. Instantly I felt that familiar pre-expedition excitement. Ian and Gobeze were laughing lightly and wiping dry mud from the car. As Bhanti sang and cleaned his gun, swifts called high above us, too high to see, yet clearly audible. On the ground near our moving shadows lay a long, metal pole, glinting like a sceptre in the sun. It looked ceremonial and splendid, fashioned for a great event. I walked over and raised it high with both hands like an Olympic torch. I imagined its tip aflame: a beacon of discovery and singular importance to humankind. I pictured it covered in skins and fur, strands of beads, perhaps even feathers. I looked at Gobeze, who had made us this special net on the longest pole I had ever seen, – and we all laughed together as it fluttered above us in the breeze – made of those same mosquito nets I had seen in the town.

Then we started back up towards the plain. Effortlessly and quietly, our shadows became the car's shadow, our movements coalesced into the car's movement, and our thoughts seemed to become the car as it headed forward, following its own tracks in the mud, following the past. Water in the tracks mirrored the sky and we appeared to float forward on clouds. Louder birds moved across us in the trees, brighter greens moved across us in the many leaves; then a stronger blue moved in the sky, wide views seemed to widen and all was more welcoming.

We moved through the forest, river, hills and valleys, back through our memories and our understandings. The journey seemed oddly quicker. High things seemed less high, beautiful things more beautiful, nature more natural. Happiness seemed surer. I looked ahead at Nechisar as its softness rolled towards me. On the curves of the plain the white grasses shone in the afternoon sun. Standing at the beginning of it all, on the line where our black track made a hard edge to the whites of the place, was the shape of a black boy. He was a little boy among bigger and taller boys, but he stood differently, with a wise smile and a sense of belonging to the place that showed him beyond his years. In one hand he held a spear and in the other an AK-47 (the gun of African liberation, the gun of child soldiers and sadness). The spear was ten times his height and reminded me of Gobeze's net. It was an important, ancient spear that belonged to the place and to the boy, piercing the sky in an oddly wise and welcoming way, so unlike the machine gun. The boy smiled, his big teeth white like the grass although stained red-brown at the gums, giving his smile the uniqueness of his spear. When he laughed for us, the other boys laughed. Gerry went and spoke to them and they welcomed us. They were cattle herders who had watched us from a far hill the previous day and were happy to see us again. Africa can teach us to share, to look with sincere eyes and remember everyday things, new things and new people. And I felt how a smile could talk.

We said goodbye to the honest boys and continued down onto the Nechisar Plains. The car pushed forward into the grass like a gazelle, and we were among the creatures of the plain again. Small herds of antelope raised their heads briefly as we passed, white below as if reflecting the grass. Dennis and Gerry unfolded our map on the back seat, crackling as we bumped along. A black circle marked the spot we were looking for.

'There's my nightjar tree,' I said.

Dennis grinned and folded the map as we changed direction towards the tree. It seemed bigger in the daytime, taller and sturdier, tall like a spear.

The darkness came suddenly before I noticed the dusk, as if the sun had become the moon. It seemed very close and personal, looming nurturingly, and I knew then why the moon in fables is so often female.

The moonlight reflected off many whites – even the antelopes' bellies – and our big shadow stretched as we stood together listening for birds. Bhanti held his gun; Dennis held his binoculars; Gerry and Gobeze held the net. The different nightjars began to call. We switched on the spotlights and set off slowly, scanning intensely for eyeshine.

Then the moon snuggled up to a cloud and buried itself, content as a bird in its nest. The darkness was immediate. Only the glow of the moon's silhouette remained, and everywhere white turned to silver. Like the edge of our shadow, the bright edge of the cloud was furry and blurry, reaching wisps into the darkness, all drifting slowly in a single direction.

'Nightjar!' I said, loud yet restrained. I shook my

torch slightly to show which light was mine. The other torch beams turned and began to cluster and criss-cross, weaving and plaiting the ground like straw matting.

Then the bird lifted. As we watched its wings unfold, white patches flashed like billboards. Our bird!

It flew out of the crossed beams and was gone. Temporarily, I hoped. I had noticed its downward arc out of the light. Down meant we still had a chance. I suspected it had landed further up the track, slightly to our left perhaps a hundred metres on, where the plain lifted slightly like a kink in the night. Perhaps, perhaps the ground still held our treasured bird for us, patiently as one might hold something very important for a friend.

Gobeze inched us forward. I shone and scanned, aiming as far ahead as it would reach, pushing my balance to the limit, unable to restrain myself as I stretched towards the hill. The beam illuminated beyond the glow of the car's headlights, animating the land in discs. Rocks, pebbles, bushes and grass clumps scurried theatrically across brief little stages, running towards us, motile. Yellow tussocks followed yellow pebbles, yellow earth and yellow sand scampered behind, all bringing the bird closer, I hoped, as if on a mass migration down the hill. The flat yellow plain that kinked upwards bobbed, its many little shapes floating on an invisible blanket being pulled towards us as the ground approached in circles of yellow. In one of the circles something twinkled like a star – like a soccer star juggling and dribbling the colour white.

'Nightjar,' I said.

'Nightjar,' said Dennis.

'Nightjar-jar-jar, ar, ar,' joked Gerry, his timing so spontaneous and surprising that I laughed very briefly, and it helped.

The eyes looked at me as if detached, strapped on like discs, reflecting the light from my torch like road signs on a hill. But these were no passive reflectors. These were nightjar eyes, organs of extreme perfection: large shiny globes densely lined with sensory receptors so exceptionally sensitive to low levels of light in the world of the night: absorbing it, regulating it, focusing, adjusting, filtering, refracting, converting it into images and transmitting it, preparing it for view, filing it, ordering it for perception, for interpretation and understanding. Everything about a nightjar is secondary to its eyes – even its beak, its body, its wings – on the ground a nightjar *is* its eyes.

I looked at the reflections shining brighter than my light. They seemed to glow from behind with an internal light, an ancient, evolutionary light – the light of day and night, of cycles, of time, of the history of vision – except now they reflected it all to me, almost superficially: such a new and coincidental use, almost inappropriate and disrespectful, almost an abuse of use.

I will never forget those eyes and what they meant to me in that moment: they gave the bird to me. Among the pebbles and the grass it sat for me, flat and huddled on the hill, completely still. It did not sit expectantly or nervously. It sat simply in response to the light, for itself, for its situation.

I never saw Ian, Gerry, Dennis or Gobeze get out of the vehicle; I saw only their backs moving darkly up the hill. Only Bhanti remained inside, baffled by our interest in so puny a bird. Ian held the horizontal net pole in one hand with his binoculars slung from a shoulder, Dennis carried his binoculars and Gobeze shone a torch. Gerry walked behind, filming the unfolding scene, the shapes of the others silhouetted against my light with the yellow bits of the hill as his stage. I climbed on top of the vehicle, holding the bird in the light, directing the team towards it.

From the roof I could see the bird clearly on the pebbles; the others could see only grass, their ankles disappearing as they walked. Depth was deceptive with grass against grass, flat and staggered like yellow cardboard cut-outs. As Ian became yellow, I shouted for him to move out of the light. Then Gerry became yellow and crackled sideways into the grass as I shouted, his arms still outstretched and filming as the camera directed him.

'Stop, Ian!' I called. '*There*,' I urged, inarticulate

in my panic. 'About two metres ahead,' I corrected.

Suddenly Ian stopped, flushing a flurry of moths into the light as if the whole plain was trying to lift into the sky. Deftly he began to manoeuvre the long pole through his hands, like a mime artist pretending to climb horizontally. Steadily the pole lengthened in front of him, until finally the dangling net at its tip turned yellow.

Gently he lifted it high.

Whoosh! He whipped it down onto the yellowest part of the ground, onto the centre of it. And our bird lifted.

It was a momentous moment, sudden and decisive, a moment that could occur only once; a reckoning beyond our control. One can prepare for such a time – if one has known such a moment before – or just wait and see, just let it come; like a famous explorer on the tip of a ship long ago, awaiting new currents and winds, new routes, new feelings, new answers. But there must always be a first time for such moments, where one has no choices, no options, no way to prepare. I stood on top of the car like an ocean explorer and watched that moment come to me.

The Nechisar Nightjar was gone. It had escaped our light.

Nothing remained but the stillness and the empty net in the yellow light. In my excitement I had viewed this net as a sceptre, a ceremonial torch, a spear, as hope incarnate. Now it was just a net.

But there are different ways to catch a bird. And in our own way we had caught it.

Gobeze started the motor again and we set out in pursuit once more. But our prize eluded us. Our bird had flown.

At last it was time for us to turn around and descend. We had reached the end of our journey, the end of the road. Coming down from our great high, the plain became flat again, no longer bent upwards like an open hand, and the ground began to fall.

We had not captured the bird, nor photographed it as we had planned. Our only real record of it now lay in our notebooks and our memories. It was good enough for me, for my bird list and my birdwatching. But it was not good enough for the headlines, for ornithology or for the international birdwatching community. Nor was it really good enough for the significance of the occasion.

We had wanted to give them more. In honesty, we had wanted more for ourselves too: recognition and praise from other birdwatchers, certainly, but more particularly to provide new support and knowledge to the Cambridge Expedition Team, as a thank-you, as an honouring and a completion their discovery.

As we went down towards the town, away from the wildness, we slowly raised ourselves up. We shook each other's hands. Then, feeling somehow that this was not intimate enough, we hugged each other too. Gerry raised his arm and gave Ian a high five. Bhanti was smiling too, happy that we were happy, happy to be heading back. I looked at his gun wedged between his hand and his knees, potent, well used and ready – and I thought about rareness. To me Bhanti was a sign like the net and the spear, a bridge that lived at the edge of Africa where forests end and people begin. He lived on the outskirts of where rareness begins.

A hippo emerged from the thicket ahead, pink and out of place, briefly caught in our headlights as it ran in jerky wobbles before the blackness absorbed it once more, leaving stretched footprints in the mud. We felt bizarrely enlightened: a hippo on a steep mountain slope so far from the lakes below where we had assumed it belonged – a sage reminder of the vast unknowns. As we moved down into the deeper darkness of the forest, down through the leaves and the river, every slow kilometre seemed to leave the moon behind, disconnecting us from the wildness of the plain.

But we had seen the rarest bird on earth. No one had seen it before, at least not scientists or birdwatchers, not those for whom rareness is a way of seeing – perhaps even saving – our wild world. Now the Nechisar Nightjar was known to live, to be more than just a wing. And like the hippo on the mountain, our sighting had changed what it was forever.

My birdwatching had made me a student of

movement and change; this is the very essence of wilderness for me. All around, birds moved with the seasons: migrating, flocking in winter and pairing in summer; moulting, donning mating plumage; nesting, singing.... And through birds I watched the sun alternate with the moon, days lengthen and shorten, warm days become cold, landscapes change colour and then change back again. Much of this change is repetitive, comfortingly predictable and regenerative. Trees grow taller, then fall, then grow anew, and where there are trees there are birds. Even the ocean rhythms, the tides and the currents, are unlocked through birds. Change is always expected and its cyclical constancy makes it almost invisible, yet it is always there: in the shadows, the sounds, the movements of birds.

But the sighting of the Nechisar Nightjar had brought a new type of change, unlike my sightings of other birds. Seeing it had instantly redefined its rareness: we had made it less rare. Knowing that it was extant, that it inhabited the remote plains of that place, part of a small remote population, perhaps even safely remote – all of this knowledge removed from it the title of Rarest of the Rare. The Nechisar Nightjar was now infinitesimally less rare, nudged almost undetectably off its throne. Its rareness moved with the creak of a widening continent; a delicate, yet powerful and inevitable shifting.

The village of Arba Minch lay in front of us, in the dark hollow of a hill, a hill-hole like the eye-socket of a dragonfly. The village turned and stared in many little lights, rare and precious electric lights under which its inhabitants gathered in groups to talk. I looked at Ian as we drove forward, his face bouncing in the lights of the village. And he was smiling. I remembered the day I had first met him many years earlier. The memory was very special, very clear, from a time when he had been to me only a famous face on the back of bird books, only a name. Now, in this place, he became suddenly familiar, alive; from being imagined long ago to being present, from being wondered about to being remembered – never ordinary, but forever different.

I looked down at the bird book on my lap, at the words and the images. And I thought of what it is to really watch, to really see.

BIBLIOGRAPHY

Arthur, W (2006) *Creatures of Accident: The Rise of the Animal Kingdom*, Hill and Wang, New York.

Belozerskaya, M (2006) *The Medici Giraffe: And Other Tales of Exotic Animals and Power*, Little, Brown Company, New York.

BirdLife International (2012). *IUCN Red List for Birds*, Downloaded from http://www.birdlife.org on 5 February 2012.

Brown, J (2006) *Darwin's Origin of Species: A Biography*, Atlantic.

Brumm, H, Farrington, H, Petren, K and Fessl, B (2010). Evolutionary Dead End in the Galapagos: Divergence of Sexual Signals in the Rarest of Darwin's Finches. *PLoS ONE*, 5 (6), pp.1–7.

Butchard, S (2007) Birds to Find: A Review of 'Lost', Obscure and Poorly Known African Bird Species, *Bulletin of African Bird Club*, 14 (2), pp. 139–157.

Cleere, N (2010) *Nightjars, Potoos, Frogmouths, Oilbirds and Owlet-Nightjars of the World*, Wild Guides Ltd, Hampshire.

Collar, N et al. (2008) Type, Locality, Habitat, Behaviour, Voice, Nest, Eggs and Plight of the Sidamo Lark, *African Bird Club*, 15 (2), pp. 180–90.

Coyne, JA (2010) *Why Evolution is True*. Oxford University Press, Oxford.

Darwin, C (2004) *The Origin of Species*, Castle
Books. (Originally published 1859).

Dawkins, R (2009) *The Selfish Gene*, Oxford
University Press, New York.

D'Orso, M (2002) *Plundering Paradise: The Hand
of Man on the Galapagos Islands*, Perennial, New
York.

Fernald, RD (1997) The Evolution of Eyes, *Current
Opinion in Neurobiology*, 10, pp. 444–50.

Forster, RG and Kreitzman, L (2009) *Season of Life:
The Biological Rhythms That Enable Living
Things to Thrive and Survive,* Profile Books,
London.

Gollop, JB, Barry, TM and Iversen, EH (1986)
Eskimo Curlew: A Vanishing Species?, Nature
Saskatchewan, Natural History Society, Regina,
Canada.

Hayman, P, Marchant, J, Prater and T (1986) *Helm
Identification Guides: Shorebirds*, A&C Black,
London.

Jackson, MH (2008) *Galapagos: A Natural History*,
University of Calgary Press, Ontario, Canada.

Juniper, T and Parr, M (2003) *Parrots: A Guide to
the Parrots of the World*, Christopher Helm,
London.

Koppel, D (2006) *To See Every Bird on Earth: A
Father, a Son and a Lifelong Obsession*, Penguin,
London.

Margulis, L (1998) *The Symbiotic Planet: A New Look at Evolution*, Weidenfeld & Nicolson, New York.

Miller, RK (2007) *Finding Darwin's God: A Scientist's Search for Common Ground between God and Evolution*, HarperCollins, New York.

Palmer, D (2006) *Seven Million Years: The Story of Human Evolution*, Phoenix, London.

Paz, O (1990) *The Monkey Grammarian*, Arcadia, New York.

Quammen, D (2007) *The Kiwi's Egg: Charles Darwin & Natural Selection*, Weidenfeld & Nicolson, London.

Reed, CEM and Murray, DP (1993) *Threatened Species Recovery Plan Series No.4: Black Stilt Recovery Plan (Himantopus novaezealandiae)*, Dept. of Conservation, NZ.

Rothenberg, D (2006) *Why Birds Sing: One Man's Quest To Solve An Everyday Mystery*, Penguin, London.

Sinclair I and Ryan P (2010) *Birds of Africa South of the Sahara*, 2nd edn, Struik, Cape Town.

Stafford, E (2012) *Walking the Amazon: 860 Days*, Ebury Publishing, London.

Stresemann, E (1975) *Ornithology: From Aristotle to the Present*, Harvard University Press, MA.

Tinbergen, N (1989) *The Study of Instinct*, Oxford University Press, Oxford.

Ward, P (1995) *The End of Evolution: Dinosaurs, Mass Extinction and Biodiversity*, Weidenfeld & Nicholson/Orion.

Watson, L (1979) *Lifetide*, Hodder and Stoughton, London.

Wilson, EO (2003) *The Future of Life*, Abacus, London.

Wilson, EO (2006) *The Creation: An Appeal to Save Life on Earth*, Norton & Co, New York.

Voigt, F and Hamer, M (2000) *Taxonomy & Systematics: The Backbone of Biodiversity Knowledge*, University of KwaZulu-Natal, South Africa.

Internet References

http://www.nwf.org/nationalwildlife/article.
  cfm?articled=678&issueId=15

http://en.wikipedia.org/wiki/Po'ouli

http://www.alvinpowell.com/

http://www.post-gazette.com/
  healthscience/20020224hawaiibirds0224p3.asp

http://www.loe.org/shows/segments.
  htm?programID=08-P13-00031&segmentID=5